The Practical Enneagram

Your Complete Self-Discovery & Spiritual Growth Workbook To Discover Your Enneagram Type, Understand All 9 Enneatypes & Deepen Your Relationships

By Sasvata Sukha

Contents

Chapter 1: Enneagram Essence & History

History, Roots & Origins

The Enneagram is a powerful tool and system for personal development, spiritual growth, and transformation. It is based on a belief in there being 9 main types of the human personality. These personality types are known as "Enneatypes," each of the 9 have their own unique qualities and characteristics. Most people identify with one primarily, however will resonate with a few. You can look to the Enneagram to discover and explore your strengths, gifts, likes, talents, and positive attributes. But the Enneagram also shows your shadow personality and self, negative traits, and potential flaws & follies, which can lead to considerable self-realization and growth. Your inner workings and desires including your hidden emotions, feelings and needs are brought to light through the wisdom of the Enneagram. It is essentially a type of system that describes the human personality in a way which can lead to spiritual awakening and awareness, whilst simultaneously sparking profound internal shifts and alignment onto our life path or purpose. Both grounding- connecting to our bodies and the earthly realm- and connection to Spirit and the higher self are available. Everyone has a specific and unique personality type (your primary type) and this further extends into the other personality types, therefore you can embody different aspects, traits and positives and negatives from the other 8 types. Yet you will be defined as having one main type. For example, if you resonate with type 2 personality you will be called "type 2," but you may still feel an affinity with types 1, 5 and 9, for example.

This unique system of self-discovery stems from the Greek "ennea," meaning *nine*, and also the Greek "grammos." Grammos translates as a 'written symbol,' so this can shed some insight into the nature of the Enneagram itself. It's like a self-contained healing system. More specifically- it is a *nine-point system,* and this provides deep insight; in numerology 9 is the number of completion. The Enneagram is further represented by a *circle* connecting the nine types in a nine-point diagram, which represents patterns of thinking, feeling, perceiving and relating to others, in addition to root struggles, predictions surrounding behavior and emotions, and virtually all aspects of one's life decisions and choices. The presence of a circle is significant as a circle symbolizes the cyclic nature of self, existence, and being. The Enneagram as a holistic system is a modern synthesis of a variety of ancient wisdoms, metaphysical teachings, and esoteric schools of thought. Religious and/or spiritual traditions also shape the meanings of the Enneatypes and its roots and history in essence.

Oscar Ichazo, one of the main figures paramount in the creation and spreading of the Enneagram as a system for healing and self-development, is someone you should be aware of, even if mildly. Oscar Ichazo was born in Bolivia and raised there and in Peru... He travelled through Asia, where he acquired a lot of his wisdom and esoteric perspectives before returning back to South America to create the foundation of his teachings. This "foundation" was an educational system to all that he learned, and, after some time, it finally became the 'Arica School.' The methods and teachings shared in this Arica School were based on the idea and practice of *self-realization*, further including a range of wisdoms and areas of self-exploration from psychology, metaphysics, spirituality, cosmology, and eastern religions. The intention of this was to bring about transformation and change in human consciousness. Amongst the teachings of his school and educational framework was the symbol of the Enneagram. The Enneagram symbol itself has its roots in antiquity-

classical times and ancient past also birthed from civilization before the Middle Ages. The symbol can actually be traced back as far as the times of Pythagoras, and it was reintroduced to the modern world by someone called George Gurdjieff, an inner work school founder who taught primarily sacred dance and movement (with the Enneagram symbol used in each). This is quite significant when analyzing the purpose and power of the Enneagram for self-discovery.

Sacred dance and movement may not initially be thought of as 'intrinsic' or closely tied to the Enneagram, as the system was built from religious, spiritual and philosophical/esoteric principles and avenues. But sacred dance and movement is a form of self-expression and deep sensuality. It is self-intimacy, in its roots, and a way to get in tune with one's innermost feelings and emotions, bodily needs, and physical sensations. Soul is able to be expressed with dance and spirit is better able to flow, thus, this makes the dancer or sacred mover a spiritual wisdom seeker. The Enneagram can be seen as the perfect philosophy to this form of self-expression. And our logic ties in perfectly with George Gurdijieff's intentions. His methods of involving the Enneagram symbol were intended to connect participants directly to the essence of this ancient symbol, also allowing them to become in

4

tune with their senses and inner feelings. One thing to note, however; unlike the system of the Enneagram shared today, Gurdjieff did not develop or teach the *personality system* also known as the *Enneatypes*.

The exact origins of the Enneagram are somewhat unknown and also a slight mystery. It is believed that this unique system for self-development has its roots back in Ancient Greece. This is mainly due to the origins of the word itself. However, it is a synthesis of a number of religious traditions including Judaism, Buddhism, Taoism, Christianity, Hinduism, Islam, and Greek philosophy. The Enneagram is not religious strictly speaking, but it is more spiritual and esoteric. It can be seen as spiritual, however, due to the innate level of spiritual awakening and transformation that naturally arises with learning about yourself in relation to the personality types. Furthermore, the person responsible for bringing the Enneagram to the Western World, George Gurdjieff, was a mystic (to some extent!). Arguably, he also acted as a "bridge" or messenger between ancient times and new, he was deeply philosophical and focused on the sacredness of life. Although George Gurdjieff is said to have played a fundamental role in the Enneagram's emergence the finding and creation of the 9

Enneatypes was down to Oscar Ichazo. On the topic of esotericism and spirituality, Ichazo actually taught a system of 108 Enneagrams in Africa known as 'Enneagons.' If you have read 'Third Eye Awakening' or know anything about yogic philosophy, you will know that 108 is a very significant number. Quite simply, 108 is believed to connect you to your source of power, the higher self, and to your crown chakra through spiritual illumination. It is rather fascinating to think that the less known system of the Enneagram has a branch that teaches 108 types! In America and the West only four main Enneagons remain, and these are the *Holy Ideas*, *Virtues*, *Passions,* and *Ego-Fixations*, which we explore later.

Ichazo's perception of the Enneagram as being a way to discover and explore the human soul, psyche and self, links to its potential and believed origins. The basis of the Enneagram in particular the four Enneagons tie in closely to mystical and philosophical traditions. Many teachings from Buddhism, Taoism and Christianity share strong similarities with the beliefs and teachings contained in the Enneagram; not the Enneagram as a symbol, but the Enneagram as a system taught today- the one with the 9 personality types. The idea and concept of 9 divine forms links to Plato's Divine Forms or Platonic Solids, which are based on the idea of there being essential qualities of existence that cannot be reduced or broken down further. Well, the same is true for the 9 Enneatypes. In Interviews with Ichazo[1] the following was shared by the founder himself:

"We have to distinguish between a man as he is in essence, and as he is in ego or personality. In essence, every person is perfect, fearless, and in a loving unity with the entire cosmos; there is no conflict within the person between head, heart, and stomach or between the person and others. Then something happens: the ego begins to develop, karma accumulates, there is a transition from objectivity to subjectivity; man falls from essence to personality." (Interviews with Ichazo, page 9, retrieved from The Enneagram Institute, 2019).

Christian mystics throughout time and history have also come up with many concepts and advocations regarding the divine, and the divinity within the ego- or "ego consciousness." This can be seen in the "7 Deadly Sins" similar to the modern-day Enneagrams' "Ego- Fixations," and "Passions." The 7 Deadly Sins of anger, pride, envy, avarice,

---

[1] The Enneagram Institute. (2019). *Traditional Enneagram (History) — The Enneagram Institute.* [online] Available at: https://www.enneagraminstitute.com/the-traditional-enneagram [Accessed 1st October 2020].

gluttony, lust and sloth actually began as *nine* forms and variations, yet over time and during their travels from Greece to Egypt reduced down to seven. The Kabbalah teachings from mystic Judaism and the Kabbalah itself contains the main principle of the ancient "Tree of Life." The *Tree of Life* is said to be a *map* presenting specific patterns into human consciousness, the ego, and psyche. All in all, it would seem the Enneagram has been built from fundamental and key archetypes of the human psyche, self, and collective consciousness energy field.

The Power of the Enneagram (Benefits & Applications)

Here we explore some of the main benefits and effects of using the Enneagram for self-exploration, healing, personal transformation, and spiritual growth.

1. Becoming aware of "blind spots"

Firstly, the Enneagram can help you to become more objectively aware of your personality "blind spots," which includes recognizing your shadow aspects and further learning to overcome them. We all have a shadow, or dark, and a light side. The day flows into night just as both the Sun and Moon shine light on our world, the Sun, of course, representing the conscious and the Moon the subconscious (or unconscious). Darkness and light simultaneously exist within and without/around. So many traditions, teachings and spiritual schools of thought speak of En*light*enment- it is finding the light within. The shadow self and personality are integral to our core personality and inner natures. Knowledge is power; therefore, the Enneagram provides great wisdom regarding your own flaws and areas for self-development, our weakness and follies. 'Blind spots!' As they are literally in the dark, subconscious or unconscious realms.

2. Divinity and Self-realization

Philosophers and teachers have always spoken of the divine aspect of man, and the self and psyche, and this is true since ancient times and times of antiquity. Transcendental states- or advanced and higher states of consciousness- can be reached; the Enneagram's teachings and aspects of the Holy Ideas and Virtues complement this, further shining a light onto the inner workings of the soul, self, and psyche. The spiritual and religious roots shared in the previous section outline how closely connected the Enneagram is to cosmic and universal symbolism-divine recognition and a higher consciousness. The more you read on and explore the Enneatypes, and the Holy Ideas, Passions, Ego-fixations and Virtues, the more you will understand and see this.

3. The ability to *Know thyself*

The personality types themselves allow you to get in tune with your true self, 'know thyself,' and shine by integrating your qualities and strengths while working to transcend your shadow. Self-love, healthy self-esteem, self-worth, and self-empowerment are all able to be embodied and increased through the wisdom of the Enneagram. Understanding yourself deeper, better, and more profoundly are other key benefits, and self-evolution and the expansion of talents, abilities and unique soul gifts too. Strength and personal empowerment can arise through "*knowing thyself*"- a term and state of awareness often associated with systems for growth and self-evolution. This encourages you to work consciously and with mindful self-talk (self-communication, transparency, and honesty) on parts of your personality that may have previously inhibited your ability to live a harmonious, healthy life. Self-love and self-care are the foundations of life, yet without education and intellectual understanding (wisdom, knowledge, learning) these cannot be properly applied. Honest and authentic self-analysis and choosing to see both the dark and light aspects of our personalities equally; with acceptance and taking steps to balance them, opens one up to new realms of opportunity and potential.

4. Similarities to Carl Jung's 'Universal Archetypes'

The personality types or Enneatypes are like an omniscient torch lighting up hidden aspects of the self, of yourself. Just like other theories and perspectives regarding consciousness and the subconscious mind, the Enneagram is an important tool for self-discovery. *Carl Jung*'s "Universal Archetypes," for example, are very similar to the ideas and concepts contained within the Enneagram. As a Personality identification system, the Enneatypes provide a foundation to work from- they show you your strengths, talent, likes, dislikes, weaknesses etc., as already established. Carl Jung was a Swiss psychologist and psychiatrist who believed that we all have *shared archetypes* inherent within the collective consciousness. These were universal archetypes true to us all. He also advocated that we all have a subconscious, conscious, and unconscious mind, which is significant when we understand the Enneagram further. The point is, we can look to the various other philosophical teachings regarding the psyche, self, and consciousness in itself to understand the Enneagram further, and vice versa. Carl Jung's universal archetypes for one help to provide insight and self-awareness with our wants, needs, weakness, strengths, hidden talents and abilities, soulful urges and desires... They also assist us in learning about our shadow- just like the Enneagram deals with the Ego-Fixations and Passions- and thus act as a catalyst for healing and spiritual self-evolution.

5. **Health, vitality, and longevity**

Another key benefit of the Enneagram is the effects it has on health, vitality and longevity. Discovering your true self and core personality through your Enneatypes opens doorways to deeper understanding and self-awareness, which in turns creates opportunities for change and transformation. With this comes emotional healing and healing on the mental, spiritual, physical and psychological planes. What can manifest is unification and harmony of *all* aspects of self. Mind, body & spirit and harmony/balance/unity on the mental, emotional, physical, and spiritual planes. This also leads to soul identification and healing, and this further opens pathways to karmic and ancestral healing, letting go of past pains, and healing from old wounds. Any one piece of insight and information passed on through the Enneagram can create ripples of positive change and transformation. We are more than a physical body; thus, health is holistic. On the spiritual, etheric, and astral planes there is a part of ourselves- our true selves- existing and interacting with our daily selves as well, so this means new potential into longevity can arise when we activate our subtle selves. Some of the healthiest people on the planet are the ones who eat plant-based, meditate and do yoga, tai chi and qi gong, and recognize the power of spirit.

6. The 'Higher Self' and Enlightenment

Linked to the last point and expanding on from the subtle energy bodies; the higher self, also known as the higher mind, is connected to embodying a spiritual energy and awareness. Higher self-awareness links to the Third Eye chakra, and this process of awakening initiates through specific 'self-realizations,' or recognitions of self. Well, the Enneagram brings many of these. Many people assume you need to live in a monastery, meditate with monks, or engage in copious amounts of self-healing or spiritual development exercises to awaken your chakras- or in this case specifically, the third eye. But this is only one aspect. *Knowledge is power*. Sometimes reading something that the intuitive mind knows to be true sparks deep levels of understanding and awareness. Words act as blueprints; they activate consciousness in a profound way. And this is true even if we can't rationalize or see something logically; intuition is an inner knowing, it's our *inner voice*. So, learning about the Enneagram is a form of healing and higher self-alignment in itself. Enlightenment is intrinsically connected with knowledge of the divine.

Furthermore, the lower self can be seen as the shadow self and the higher self as the divine, non-human self. We integrate the teachings of the lower/shadow self (Ego-Fixations, Passions) and evolve to the wisdom and gifts of the higher self/enlightened self (Holy Ideas, Virtues). This doesn't mean the shadow self is 'wrong' or 'evil,' it just means we seek to transmute and alchemize certain parts of our personality into something more encompassing and helpful. Actually, the shadow self is essential for creative self-expression and emotional connection, just as the lower self teaches us about our primal passions and animalistic urges!

The higher self can be seen as a portal to higher states of awareness, which includes pathways to healing and wholeness. It also provides a bridge to a higher power, such as God, the universe, source, or Spirit. It can connect you to your psychic and intuitive abilities and senses and is subsequently a link to all spiritual or "supernatural" abilities; precognition, the "4 clairs"- clairvoyance, clairsentience, claircognizance and clairaudience; intuition, telepathy, the ability to perceive subtle energy, and dream states.

7. Soul Purpose and True Path

Finally, self-discovery through the Enneagram personality types aligns you with your soul purpose, path and truth- your true north. Destiny and legacy are words often linked to the Enneagram as a system of spiritual illumination and healing. We all have a calling in the world, a unique "soulprint"- a perfect vibratory blueprint of our essence and self. It is important to note that "destiny" here is not seen as something completely above and beyond us or the human self. The human experience is a combination of both light and dark, shine and shadow, and the higher self and lower self. Your "soulprint" or unique blueprint of self, therefore, is these aspects balanced, integrated and harmonized, it is a grounded version of our higher selves. And this is what the Enneagram aims to achieve. Once this has been attained and the dualistic, yet complementary forces embodied, this is where you can truly begin your journey integrating your Personality type, and the subsequent purpose or life path involved with mastering yourself. New heights can be reached, new opportunities can arise, and new and advanced or evolved levels of awareness can be attained, in addition to new chapters embarked on (or reinforced if you're already on your path).

As the Enneagram teaches, we have a primal, inner animal and ego- driven self. "Destiny" is the holistic human experience in its entirety, and understanding the quality of *intuitive wisdom* and how it can be enhanced, developed and embodied- through the Enneagram's teachings- is one sure way to align you onto your life purpose and true path. Through learning about your core struggles, passions, holy ideals, and virtues you can come to terms with those parts of yourself you may not want to accept, and the most brilliant and beautiful aspects you have yet to fully embody and balance. Spiritual self-development and self-mastery, which is otherwise known as mastery of your mind, body, emotions, and spirit, can only be experienced once we have done the "inner work," got completely honest and real with ourselves, and treated our own lives with authenticity, open vulnerability and an utter willingness to learn and evolve. Of course, we also need to be open mentally and on a soul or spiritual level to the possibilities and dimensions of spirit, or spiritual awareness and knowing. The fact that having or resonating with a "type" doesn't mean you are boxed into one personality, i.e. you can be one type but share aspects of another, or many others, simultaneously; means that resonating with a type signifies the tendencies from that personality manifest stronger, and that you are more prone to the positive and negative aspects than the other Enneatypes. So, this in itself gives you key clues and prompts regarding significant life decisions, correct routes, and pathways to choose- most in alignment with your soul and spirit- and where you can naturally thrive and shine. (And simultaneously where you may potentially fall or fail.) Your type is your "basic personality type" acting as a foundation and core aspect of your true nature.

Chapter 2: 'Enneatypes'- 9 Personality types

Each personality type relates to relationships, career, love, family & friendships, health, spirituality, and virtually all major areas for self-development and life exploration. Let's now look at each of the 9 Enneatypes. Please note that this a very *detailed* analysis of the 9 personality types, quite possibly all you will ever need to know. It also serves as a foundation to the other two books in this series.

You can look to the *Levels of Development* to understand where you might be on your current stage of development, or where you were in the past. There are also insights into your *Shadow Traits*, negative aspects of the personality type.

***

Type 1: The Reformer

Type 1's are also known as 'Reformers' and idealists. They are perfectionists with a sense of purpose, dedication, and commitment. Self-control and integrity define the type 1 personality, and there is a firm understanding of wrong from right. Morals and ethics, notions of good and evil, and combining intuition with practical wisdom serve a type 1 well. They are disciplined, idealistic and principled- if this is your personality type you can generally be trusted by colleagues, partners, friends, and family. This is truer when older and matured. Your main qualities include honesty, responsibility, dependability, and integrity. On a higher emotional level and frequency, you possess great serenity and can let go of things others' may not be able to do so easily. Grounded, practical, and sociable with strong organization skills, you can achieve great success when applying yourself and staying committed to chosen paths. Purpose defines you. There's a sense of mission.

Type 1 personality is conscientious and ethical. In work and professional situations, you are seen as trustworthy and dependable. Bosses or peers often look to you to get the job done or to come up with innovative and strong solutions. Problem-solving, common sense, organization and order are some of your strongest assets. At home, you are very practical and reliable. Your lover or children know, over time, that you are the one to look towards for all matters of finances, responsibilities, and domestic affairs. As an idealist you're also creative with a unique way of seeing things. You may be artistic or creatively gifted. Many type 1s enjoy finding creative and original activities to introduce to the family. You thoroughly love social dos and affairs too. You're loved by friends and family for your ability to put on a fabulous party, provide food and drinks, and create joy and fun for those you love. Merged with this is the fact that you unconsciously play the role of teacher- you're a way shower with a powerful spirit.

You're an advocate for change. Teaching and speaking comes naturally to yourself as the 'Reformer' personality type, so you may find yourself working in large companies or business, charity or humanitarianism. Alternatively, you may be a motivational speaker or coach, actual teacher, or leader of an organization, corporation or non-profit. Becoming a musician, spoken word artist, entertainer or public change advocate could suit you perfectly as well. Overall, so long as you feel you are working towards something, seeking to create a better world, and using your voice to do so, you are generally happy. Because of your strong morals and ethics there's further an inspirational aspect to you... you like to inspire, uplift and enlighten through your wisdom and skill set. You're realistic, wise, discerning, and sometimes courageous in your reasoning and approach. Bravery and inner fire can lead to truly heroic and selfless acts at key moments in your life. Your key motivations in life are to improve, create change, and inspire truth. Higher ideals and a sense of 'vision' are inherent to your core programming and personality. You have high standards and, again, can be a perfectionist. Your sense of mission and devotion to a cause can make you utilize whatever resources and influence you have to create powerful change. Your energy can be quite catalytic, you believe in a higher power and like to feel and be useful.

You do like to be right too. When expressed positively and consciously, this can lead to brilliant insight and a desire for change on both an individual and collective level. You can be a real force in your industry or global communities. Practically the need to be right signifies a striving towards higher ideals and the pursuit of knowledge; higher learning features throughout your life. Consistency in your beliefs, actions and ideals is another positive trait of yours. You don't mind speaking your truth or standing up for yourself either, justifying and defending yourself comes easily. Your primary desire in life is to be good and ethical, to have integrity, and to live a balanced and true life. Your main fear is the fear of being corrupted, imperfection and giving into the "lesser" or evil/bad aspects of the self and psyche. Of course, this can have its setbacks as we explore next, but positively these manifest as a constant conscious strive for change and positive actions, self-development, and personal growth. Spiritual maturity and self-alignment can also result through self-betterment.

Type 1 Shadow Traits

Type 1's can be judgmental, intolerable, and very uncompromising. This works two ways. Firstly, you can be uncompromising to others. Once you've got an idea in your head, or believe yourself to be right, it is virtually impossible for you to release your tight grip of control. You can thus become dogmatic and pushy in your desires for 'perfection' or power. Secondly, this uncompromising aspect to your nature makes you treat yourself less than kindly. You can be very uncompassionate and hard on yourself! Type 1's are also known for a highly critical nature and can fall into resentment and uncontrollable anger if you do not learn how to express yourself. This is, of course, due to your idealistic and perfectionist nature which is a beautiful thing. But it can take a while for you to find inner balance and learn how to integrate this aspect of your personality. When functioning on a lower emotional frequency, you can become very unadaptable and immovable in your views, and this can lead to resentment and criticism.

Type 1 is mainly strong-willed with extraordinary nobility regarding morals, ethics, and all matters of integrity; yet, there is such a thing as the balance of power. This is the balance created from recognition of two sides of one's personality- the light and the darkness. Denying your darkness (shadow self) ultimately leads to it overtaking, taking precedence over your lightness (beautiful strengths and qualities). Seeking perfection 24-7 and being angry or critical when this doesn't happen means you can give into feelings of depression, anxiety, severe stress, or low moods. Minor or major health issues can arise. Stress and anxiety are the main things you need to watch out for, especially as an idealistic reformer who strives to make the world a better place. Learning how to take it easy, adopt a more laid-back and down-to-earth attitude, and simply find time for rest and relaxation are essential if you wish to find the inner balance you so desperately seek. Further, you often spend a lot of time thinking about the consequences of your actions. This has its positives- for one it makes you a better person and one who also learns from their mistakes or failures. However, it can manifest as you being 'stuck in the past.'

Not only do you have a tendency of becoming stuck in the past, but you also over-analyze and feel like you need to justify your actions when you don't. Not everyone is as idealistic or noble as you! Life isn't a race and you aren't under constant analysis. Being too self-betterment focused can make you miss out on the joys and pleasure of life, which also leads to disconnection. Disconnection from your whole, true, and holistic/balanced self and disconnection from others. To help with this, you should try replacing over-analysis of the past and consequences of your actions with *reflection.* Positive reflection, introspection, and activities like journaling, writing, and expressing yourself through music, dance, and art would help you immensely. In other words, engage in down-time where you can soul-search or view your actions and history with a more empathic and self-compassionate mindset.

You're an activist, which means you spend a lot of time relying on passion and instinct to get you through and create ripples. This is a very positive thing. Passion and instinct help you in many moments of life. *Yet*, in an effort to stay true to your principles you often suppress your instinctual drives and intuitive feelings. You consciously repress them and give into resistance, and over time this leads to unconsciously suppressing them. Your ability to act from instinct and intuitive guidance are so powerful. Try not to let logic, reason, or your desire for perfection and idealism replace the things you know to be true within. Listen to your higher self, inner voice and instincts, as this is where passion and conscious action arise. You naturally have a very strong inner compass, thus your problem lies in "being your own worst enemy," or "shooting yourself in the foot." Devolving and digressing in the name of evolution is a paradox you need to come to terms with throughout life.

So, your key shadow traits are being too strict with yourself (and others), seeking control and perfection (life is duality, perfection naturally involves imperfection!), and moving backwards and not trusting your instincts. Overthinking can be combated with more feeling, and you can do this by getting in tune with your sensuality and learning to let go, release control from time to time. When something is good, allow it to be good- don't find mistakes or imperfections that aren't there. Not only will this assist you on your life path and sense of mission, it will inspire you towards self-mastery. Self-mastery is a *balance* of mind, body, emotions and spirit. Perhaps you need to shift your focus to embody various dimensions and aspects of your true self?

Type 1s: Plato, Joan of Arc, Mahatma Gandhi, Nelson Mandela, Kate Middleton, Michelle Obama, Noam Chomsky, and Meryl Streep.

Levels of Development

Healthy Levels: -

1. **When at your Best**: You're wonderfully wise, discerning, intuitive and dependable.

25

You navigate life with ease and effortless nobility, ethics and what is right and wrong come naturally to you, and you tend to inspire others through your idealistic passions and visions. You believe in a better world and use your time to create change that will benefit others. You know when to take time for yourself and to rest & play.

2. **Slightly below your best**: You're conscientious with strong personal convictions. You've discovered your own set of beliefs and values and like to apply these within local communities and society. You're on your way to being an inspirational role model and changemaker- people recognize your gifts and ideals. You're generally mature, rational, and balanced.

3. **Nearly there**: You're considerably principled with a fair, intuitive, and practical approach and perspective to life. Truth and justice are important to you and you prefer to find constructive ways to use your time and energy. You're on a path of service and responsibility and are aware of your purpose, but you've yet to find a healthy balance. You still give into some of your shadow personality aspects (although you are aware of them).

Average levels: -

4. **On the Path**: You're dissatisfied with reality but have taken steps to change. You have some strong morals and ideals integrated, you're an idealistic visionary with a sense of righteousness. You feel it's up to you to help others and change the world. You do, however, speak in metaphor- how things "should" be and what you "ought" to do next. Your intentions are confirmed however not everything is in motion.

5. **Learning, still in the Shadow stage**: You've become orderly and well-organized with a strong sense of right from wrong. You're afraid of making mistakes, appearing wrong, or being judged- sometimes quite severely. You dislike being seen in an unfavorable light yet haven't healed your shadow self or integrated the various aspects of your personality. You're a workaholic and are prone to emotional repression and suppression, pedanticness, and fastidiousness.

6. **Devolved**: You're highly critical of others, controlling, and a clear perfectionist. You get stressed easily and sometimes lose your cool when things don't go your way. You're opinionated and intolerable at times, you nitpick others and demand a lot from them.

Unsatisfied and disorganized your life is a bit of a mess! But, you have seen the light and received a glimpse into your future, strengths, and true path. You know how things should be.

Unhealthy levels

Self-righteous, dogmatic, inflexible, and controlling. You feel you are the only one who knows the truth, or the way things should be. You're judgmental, unconsciously arrogant, preachy, and angry. You project onto others and feel you know best based on some knowledge acquired. But, your wisdom is young and you still have a lot to learn! This state can be seen as a teenager who feels they know best, without realizing just how much they have to learn. You become obsessed with the wrongdoings of others and highly hypocritical. You can even be abusive or cruel when people don't reach your morals or idealistic beliefs, condemning them for not being 'perfect.' Nervous breakdowns, depression, stress, and health problems often result in this stage of development. Obsessive-compulsive personality disorder may take hold and you are still generally in the dark as to your true power and purpose.

Type 2: The Helper

Personality type 2 is the Helper. Type 2's are generous, kind, and people-pleasing. This personality type is all about relationships; platonic friendships, family bonds, love, and romantic connections, and business partnerships. The connections one holds with others is integral to a type 2 personality. There is a strong desire to give love and be loved, to hold and be cherished. Affection favors strongly and there's nothing 'too much' for a type 2. If this is your personality type, you are more than happy to devote your time and energy to those you love and trust. You're caring, nurturing and wholly selfless. You possess extraordinary humility and modesty. You could be the most amazing musician, singer, artist, or speaker and you would down-play it- your humility and selflessness are extraordinary. You're also happy to spend a lifetime helping others, devoted to some person, organization or cause.

You like to take on the role of caregiver, nurturer, diplomat, and mediator. Many type 2's actually become counsellors, meditators, or diplomats. In personal relationships you are a natural listener, empath, and counsellor and give amazing advice. You're wise, perceptive, and generous in your observations and speech, time and energy. Speaking of empathy, type 2 is associated with the personality of the empath. You have the ability of seeing below the surface, reading between the lines, and seeing directly into people's issues and lives. Everything internal that is usually a secret, you can sense and "see" with advanced intuitive and empathic gifts. There's a psychic and spiritually perceptive aspect of the type 2 personality too. You function at a high emotional frequency. What does this mean? It signifies that you embody the unique vibration of emotional intelligence, intuition, instinct and empathy, and combine it with spiritual insight and wisdom. 'Holding space' comes effortlessly for you too, a gift and skill some people spend lots of money trying to master in the form of workshops, courses, and training programs! Holding space involves a type of presence. It's the capacity for mindful and empathic communication, truly listening without judgement, and offering advice that is wise, discerning, and perceptive.

Empathy and compassion and a genuine care for the well-being of others characterize holding space. Again, it is symbolic of empaths and as a type 2 you embody the empath nature. To hold space for another is a skill that includes evolved listening skills and an integrated sense of empathy, kindness, and nurturance- qualities you possess in abundance. You do this naturally through your diplomatic and mediating role, with friends, family, and strangers, and it is further a skill that can be mastered through grounding your compassion and advanced emotional frequency into a professional path. Type 2's are helpers, healers, caregivers, and nurturers; natural counsellors, psychics, intuitivists and warm-hearted people. Expanding on, relationships take center stage in your life. Your identity is wrapped up in the close bonds you form and keep. You believe in the power of community, friendship, soulmates, or kindred spirits. Many type 2's choose to enter into a 'power couple' relationship, a romantic bond symbolized by shared passions and interest, service, and a shared path or talent. People in a power couple have a shared sense of destiny and purpose- they embark on certain pathways and roads to help others, for example being two humanitarian or charity aid workers travelling the world together. Or two musicians inspiring others and raising the collective vibration of humanity through music.

When at your best, your self-worth and self-esteem are independent of any faulty perception, judgement or ego delusion. You may be tied into personal relationships and close emotional bonds, but you have a strong sense of self. Your strength allows you to be a support system for others, people who know you consider you a gem with pearls of wisdom and a heart of gold. Magnanimity, benevolence, generosity, and selflessness define you. You excel at making connections, empathic communication, and showing real and sincere displays of affection, care and compassion. When you balance your autonomy and self-sovereignty with your need for connection and, often, praise or approval, you can thrive in any aspect of life. You're demonstrative too, which signifies that you like to put on displays of your love, generosity, and affections. This has its positive and shadow traits. Positively, you can inspire people by showing them the true meaning of giving and kindness. Being sincere and genuine in your benevolence sparks humility and integrity, two qualities you're not short of! Your friendly and open aura nature helps others around you to bask in your unconditional love and warmth. You're sincere, somewhat spiritual, and believe in the power of soul and heart. Your basic fear can lead to self-development and working on yourself to be the best version of yourself. Your basic fear as a type 2 is the fear of being unloved, unseen, and unwanted. Also, you have issues in self-worth.

Learning how to channel this constructively allows you to open your heart to others, and vibrate at your highest- embodying the qualities of kindness, giving, empathy etc. Type 2's are natural hosts and hostesses- you're the entertainer of a party and know how to treat your guests. You can create warm, welcoming and cozy environments for others. You put people at ease with your energy and intentions. Your main motivations in life are to be able to express your feelings and create stable and loving bonds. 2 is a number of stability, security, and *duality*; finding oneness and unity within the separation and confusion. All of life involves duality and this is something you are very familiar with, even if it's on an instinctual or subconscious level. You have powerful instincts that are rooted in your connection to others. Your senses are developed and many type 2's have spiritual or psychic gifts. Clairvoyance is common as is the ability to receive wisdom and insight from your subconscious mind in dreams. Because your idea of reality is rooted in your connection to others, people, animals, nature and the planet, any sign of disconnection is a motivation factor to rise up and be centered within. You strive for inner strength and prefer to put on a brave face, even when you're feeling weak or low. You're truly a rock and a powerful support system for others, and- when at your best- you don't need the validation or recognition from others. You're happy to give from the grace and kindness of your heart.

Unselfish, altruistic, and genuine you are the personality type that most represents unconditional love. You're blessed with a refined sensuality and grace, an ability to see beyond the surface and veil of illusion (linked to number 2 being linked to relationships and duality) and a universal sense of compassion. You're invested in others and the relationships you hold close. Feeling, nurturance, caring, and devotion are all important to you whilst deep and meaningful conversation help to remind you of your connection to humanity. Without family, friendship, closeness and sharing your life would appear meaningless- and these are beautiful things. Pets, cooking, home, gardening, community and traditional values are a key part to a type 2's lifestyle.

Type 2 Shadow Traits

Your shadow traits need to be worked on, however. You can become very people-pleasing, self-sacrificing, and codependent. These are your worst personality traits and things you really need to work on if you wish to live a balanced, harmonious, and happy life. You often deny or repress your own needs to help or please everyone else. You sacrifice a lot and focus on the wellbeing of others, yet dismiss your own needs, desires, or wellbeing. This can lead to problems in health, money, wealth, career, and personal relationships. Codependency arises when you've spent so long being selfless in the name of service (help), and therefore become unconscious of the patterns emerging. You may not even recognize your own passions, ambitions, or soulful longings after a period of time. Other shadow traits to watch out for include pride, arrogance, low self-esteem and issues in self-worth and confidence.

Your primary desire in life is to be loved, give love, be cherished and appreciated; you want to be seen and known for your ability to care and provide for others.

Yet, this creates internal chaos and afflictive emotions. People-pleasing takes hold, you turn to smothering or molly-coddling- being overbearing in your love and affections. You can ironically suppress others through your need to take care of them. Nurturance transforms into interfering and meddlesome, 'babying' and intrusive patterns of behavior take hold. Alternatively, you can become possessive and obsessive, which is a direct result of the internal chaos you feel from being overbearing without consciously recognizing it. In terms of low self-esteem and self-worth, your confidence suffers drastically as a manifestation of all of these things. Instead of being seen as the beautiful, shining and generous person that you are, the people closest to you view you in a different light. This can then leave you feeling alienated or rejected. Remember that type 2 is all about relationships, connections, and duality/oneness. Self-sacrifice isn't healthy, if you want a relationship to work you must respect your own needs too. 'Give a little to give a lot' is a good mantra it would be wise to adopt.

Furthermore, there is a tendency to become fake, false or deceptive. You may give false compliments which people can sense are staged, or you might actually resort to manipulation and deception in your desire to be liked. Again, this creates disunity in your relationships. Giving from kindness and sincerity becomes replaced with doing for others in order to be needed or loved. Superficiality is a shadow aspect when you're not at your best. Subservience too. This leads to resentment! Passive aggressiveness isn't as bad as being violent or physically aggressive, but it does create inner problems and conflict. You need to be careful of repressed emotions, built up anger and frustration, and resentment which all stem from your need for love and appreciation. Learning to appreciate yourself will help you immensely- practice self-love and self-care as much as possible. Be mindful of pride, self-deception, and emotional manipulation as well. You have extraordinary levels of love and compassion, so know that your worthiness stems from your genuine intentions and selfless acts. Self-acceptance can be key to your success and health. Acknowledge your emotional needs and practice "healthy selfishness," selflessness for yourself!

Treat yourself to a massage, spa getaway, and frequent breaks. Eat healthy and high-vibration, nutritious foods to nourish yourself, and do things that you love and enjoy. Pleasure without steering to the dark side of hedonism can help you to glow and feel good within. This then allows you to give and shine externally in perfect amounts, which further sparks your ego (in a healthy way). You need to understand that it's okay to make sacrifices to please and help others- core parts of your nature and personality (of which there is no escape), but life involves *balance*. Relationships serve as a mirror to your soul, self and psyche, more so than anyone else. Positive reflection will aid you in discovering your true self and overcoming any shadow tendencies you may still be holding onto. Learn to let go of self-denial, repression, and self-judgement.

Type 2s: Paramahansa Yogananda, Desmond Tutu, Eleanor Roosevelt, Luciano Pavarotti, John Denver, Lionel Richie, Stevie Wonder, Elizabeth Taylor, and Bobby McFerrin.

Levels of Development

Healthy Levels: -

1. **When at your Best**: You're deeply empathic, humble, giving and selfless. Your life is defined by generosity and the love, care, time and energy you give to others, yet you also take care of yourself. You've learned how to balance giving with receiving

and being a support system with self-care. You're altruistic, unselfish, unconditionally loving and live life in a state of flow, gratitude, and grace.

2. **Slightly below your best**: You possess deep empathy and feel for others. You're kind and caring, compassionate, and warm-hearted. People see you as friendly and welcoming although sometimes slightly people-pleasing. Generally, you are a gift to be around.

3. **Nearly there**: You're sincere, thoughtful, considerate and open-hearted. You see the good in others and believe in the power of service, of helpfulness. You're nurturing, generous, loving and supportive of those you love. You're still dealing with the final stretches of overcoming your shadow personality traits, and are thus prone to occasional feelings of resentment, pride and self-sacrifice. You recognize these, however, and have already begun your healing journey.

Average levels: -

4. **On the Path**: You genuinely desire to be of service to others but still have a problem with people-pleasing. You can be overly friendly,

fake flattering, and slightly seductive or emotionally manipulative. You're full of good intentions and know your strengths and qualities, also having real moments of purity and sincerity shine through. You want to be closer to others and talk about love, empathy and compassion more than you embody it authentically.

5. **Learning, still in the Shadow stage**: You're overly intrusive, intimate and meddlesome. You molly-coddle, people-please, and give too much of yourself away- including your time, energy, love, and resources. You're prone to codependency and possessiveness, self-sacrifice and trying to be everything for everyone. It's hard for you to destress yet you possess integrity and a desire to be of service, even if you don't know how.

6. **Devolved**: You're arrogant, prideful, overbearing and patronizing. There is a glimmer of hope and light behind the surface- your core nature is there but not developed at all. You're overcome with feelings of self-importance and self-righteousness rooted in your desire to serve. You can be a martyr at times and assume and presume a lot. You're interested in compassion and altruistic topics, however,

and are just beginning your journey of healing and self-realization.

Unhealthy levels

Manipulative, sympathy and attention seeking, and self-serving, you have a lot of personal power but don't know how to channel it yet. Sparks of insight have come to you, possibly through meditation, books, and dreams, however you are seeking knowledge and wisdom about yourself. This time of life is most likely symbolic of mid-late teens and/or early adult years. Addictions can take hold such as food, alcohol, or medication and you resort to belittling others often. You're self-deceptive, domineering, self-entitled and seductive. You often feel abused or victimized by others too all the while not realizing the role you play in your suffering. There's a lack of self-awareness and wisdom, which leads to frequent anger and resentment. Emotions can be chaotic.

Type 3: The Achiever

Type 3 is known as the 'Achiever.' This person is driven to excel, shine, and achieve success. Personal victories, accomplishment, and fame or prestige are very important to type 3s. They possess a powerful success mindset, pragmatism, high energy levels and well-developed ambition, perseverance, and determination. Type 3s are the high-flyers and achievers of society, always seeking to better themselves through education, training programs, workshops and career development. Their career and the money they make is very important to them. Yet, they are also talented and gifted. They aren't solely driven by money or fame. If you are a type 3, you're motivated and multi-talented, disciplined and aren't shy of the spotlight. Being admired and receiving affection is okay with you- it's actually welcomed! You actively seek out the limelight and like to shine to inspire others, and to receive personal success. There is a fine balance between personal recognition and individual victory and the type of service or inspiration you provide others (when operating at your best).

You're an incredible communicator. Sharing ideas and thoughts, expressing yourself, and communicating through music, imaginative channels, or artistic modes of expression all favor well for you. You work well with others. You're a team player, knowing when to give your input and contribute to a group or shared activity. In the workplace, you are seen as a force to be reckoned with and a valuable member of the team. Energetic, charismatic, bold and with a strong life force, you take on life with enthusiasm and dedication.

Committing to a project or cause you're genuinely passionate about comes naturally to you. You are also highly adaptable and generally successful in all you put your mind to. A major strength is in your emotional connection and intelligence which you use and channel into getting things done. When at your best you exhibit an advanced level of truthfulness and wisdom and can see beyond the surface and above superficial appearances. Personal authenticity, self-autonomy and self-expression are strong and evolved. You enjoy creating opportunities and magic around you and many type 3s tend to be abundant and financially prosperous.

Multi-talented, you can thrive in the creative and artistic fields just as you can succeed in marketing or finances. You have lots of passion, so combined with your creative talents you may choose to work in media, TV and film, the Arts, or any creative or musical field. Publishing is a perfect professional path for you too. If you choose a less artistic route you can exert your creativity and innovative skills in business, marketing, I.T, technology or working your way up the ladder to manager or CEO. Referring back to emotional intelligence, and truthfulness and wisdom; you are wise, perceptive, intelligent and quite intuitive. Not typically the most intuitive personality type, you do have a connection to your inner voice and instincts. This helps you in many situations in life, both professional and personal. You like to check in with yourself when making important decisions or deciding on certain paths, and your problem-solving skills are off the chain. Emotionally mature and intelligent, your instincts can guide you and shine a light on key areas that ultimately lead to your success. They also aid in connecting you to others and creating important bonds and opportunities through business and partnership. You're bound for success and accomplishment when you open yourself up to important connections.

Adaptable, driven, self-aware and optimistic, you are charming to others. You exhibit charisma and social grace, although you have a courage and inner boldness that can sometimes make you *slightly* tactless. For the most part, you are charming and have a positive social/public image. You're equally very attractive and most likely have many admirers. You're self-assured and extremely confident- you ooze personal authority and power, which stems from your talents and unique gifts. Ambition, competence and poise define you. When you set your mind on something you are relentless in your capacity to achieve it; perseverance and inner strength are some of your greatest qualities. You're diplomatic but competitive as well. Depending on which aspect you're steering more towards, this can have some wonderful results. When you're more in tune with your diplomatic, harmony seeking, cooperative and team player side, the competitive aspect leads to your success. It acts as a 'boost' and enhancement for your strengths and qualities. At your best you're authentic, inspiring and a role model to others. Your main desire and drive in life is to feel valuable, worthy, and seen. You are open to power, fame, wealth and prestige and enjoy sharing your abundance and success with those you love. Not selfish, however not wholly selfless (like a type 2), you enjoy the finer things in light and- again- the spotlight.

Your primary fear in life is being worthless. When channeled constructively this can inspire you to new heights. You become a power-force, motivated and full of passion to follow your dreams and realize your aspirations. Professionalism and integrity are developed, you thrive in a range of roles and paths, and your creativity and intellect are second to none. Number 3 is a very creative number, signifying that you may succeed as a musician, soul singer, artist, painter, poet, author, writer, spoken word artist, entertainer, model, or actor or actress. Attention and admiration from others is a catalyst to push you to the next level, and impressing others is one of your key motivations. You can achieve great things in the world through your immense spirit, passion and heart. Type 3 is the 'star' of the world! But you're gracious and capable of deep displays of compassion and empathy too. You're certainly not heartless, soulless, or disconnected from friends, family and your community. Contributing to the world is intrinsic to your intentions for public recognition and social status, or fame or wealth; many 3s use their newfound power and status, talents of evolved gifts to help others, further becoming a way shower, teacher, or role model. Cultured, wise and gifted communicatively you believe in the extraordinary and pushing yourself to new heights within and around. *'Being the best you can be'* is your mantra throughout life.

Type 3 Shadow Traits

Your shadow personality is characterized by needing to impress others at the extent of losing yourself. You can be overly competitive, impatient, and lacking tact, grace and discernment (when at your worst). Becoming a workaholic is a key negative aspect to this personality type, so you must learn how to balance work, rest and play. Focusing too much on praise, admiration and materialism or fame, wealth and power can be one of your greatest downfalls. This is the most prominent shadow tendency of type 3. You're so high-flying and high achieving that your chase of wealth and prestige can result in unconsciously alienating those closest to you. You may become arrogant, extremely self-centered, and even narcissistic in nature. Competitiveness may result in your disconnection from communities and being the wonderful team player and asset you usually are. Instead of people gravitating towards you for motivation, seeing you as charismatic, approachable and inspiring- they instead ignore or avoid you. Your beautiful qualities can become replaced with a "darkness," and sometimes you're not entirely conscious of it.

The need for external praise can leave you out of touch and tune with your own feelings. You begin to question yourself and turn towards a mild form of narcissistic personality disorder. Friends, lovers and family don't want to be around you, and they start to see you as conceited and unattractive. You also question which role or character you should take on-self-worth diminishes and you begin to lose confidence when you give into your shadow personality traits. Using your strong sense of autonomy and personal authority to think, act and behave in a way in alignment with your true self and core talents, is overruled with allowing others to decide what is relevant and important for you. This is another key shadow trait; you place too much importance on other people's perceptions and judgements. Remember to let go of image and social persona and connect to your inner truth, essence, and emotional wisdom and intelligence. Your beautiful qualities are powerful, and they should be a priority. Allowing others to control your life and self-development (or success) through their opinions is not only counterproductive to your goals, but it also makes you be seen in a less than attractive light.

Due to your primary desire in life of being worthy, seen and recognized for your gifts and achievements, frustrations and internal emotional chaos can build up when you forget the power of self-love. You want success because you're afraid of emptiness and worthlessness, yet this leads you to 'act out.' Egotistical, narcissistic or overly self-centered displays diminish your sparkle. Self-love and self-care are placed with constant internal chatter, overthinking and negative self-talk- 'how do other people see me?' Independence and self-autonomy are reduced as a result. There's also an aspect of rushing and not thinking things through when you're attuned to the frequency of attempting to impress everyone, or be liked and loved. Your usual extraordinary communication skills and ability to charm, inspire and uplift become distorted through your fears and insecurities. Always focusing on the future goals as opposed to living in the now and being present with yourself. Manipulations and deceptions of others can interfere with your path and success when you give into too much 'future thinking.' Instincts and intuition along with emotional intelligence diminish, and you lack the confidence to make the best choices. Losing touch with yourself is the main element of all of these setbacks.

Furthermore, you need to be mindful of feelings VS thinking. Being so concerned with performance and how others see you implies that you often override your feelings, you create the belief that emotions can get in the way of your performance or success. Your success is *rooted* in your emotional intelligence, wisdom and capacity for authentic connection... try not to substitute feeling and emotion for thinking and practical action. You adapt your life to meet the expectations of others, but a lot of the time these are self-imposed expectations of how you believe other people to perceive you. It's a form of self-created illusion, a "self-created prophecy." Rest, play and chill time are really significant for your wellbeing and success. Finally, you crave acceptance on all levels; in platonic and family bonds, in friendships, in love and romance, and in career and vocation or business. Meditation, introspection, self-healing and taking time to yourself are key areas for self-improvement.

Type 3s: Arnold Schwarzenegger, Carl Lewis, Muhammed Ali, Oprah Winfrey, Deepak Chopra, Tony Robbins, Madonna, Whitney Houston, Lady Gaga, Cindy Crawford, Tom Cruise, Justin Bieber, Will Smith, Jamie Foxx, Kevin Spacey, Anne Hathaway, Reese Witherspoon, and Demi Moore.

Levels of Development

Healthy Levels: -

1. **When at your Best**: You're authentic, self-expressive, an excellent communicator, and connected to your purpose and gifts. Modest, humble, charming and friendly, people love you. They know you can inspire them and motivate them to new heights. You possess heart, spirit and soul and shine in order to be a role model in your communities. Benevolence and charity are strong too.

2. **Slightly below your best**: You're energetic, passionate, self-assured and confident. You possess high self-esteem and believe in yourself and others. You like to motivate others and enjoy using your success or social standing to benefit others in some way. Gracious, charming and adaptable, you're

competent and valued but still have some minor issues in taking it easy.

3. **Nearly there**: You're ambitious and like improving yourself. You want to be the best, and know that your purpose is tied into the work you can do to connect and uplift others. Your motivations for success aren't selfish-they're aligned with a shared sense of humanity and global society/community. At this stage you're concerned with reaching the top for personal and professional victory. There are still some shadow traits you need to work through.

Average levels: -

4. **On the Path**: You're very concerned with your performance, the way others see you, and your level of social status and success. A drive for perfection and excellence is constant, if not obsessive. But, you've seen the light and your intentions for this are positive. You're terrified of failure, however, this can lead to some strong displays of your shadow. You give into comparison and competition and are currently climbing the social ladder. You're aware of your destiny.

5. **Learning, still in the Shadow stage**: You're extremely image-conscious, ambitious and relentless in your pursuit for power and fame/success. What others think of you takes center stage in your daily life. You lose touch with your instincts and feelings, however, are pragmatic and determined, hard-working and motivated. There's still a lot to learn! You unconsciously adapt to the expectations and motivations of others, so there are problems with intimacy, authenticity, and transparency. Your communication isn't yet mastered either.

6. **Devolved**: You want to impress others, create a good impression, and won't accept failure or being seen in a less than favorable light. You resort to manipulation and twisting the truth if this happens. You're not entirely trustworthy and struggle with narcissism, grandiose self-notions, and inflated delusions of your talents, worth and achievements. You're optimistic and self-assured but have not yet become successful. *'Fake it until you make it'* is the best saying to go here! Netherthless, it can lead to disconnection from friends, family and loved ones (through arrogance, self-centeredness etc.).

Unhealthy levels

You fear failure and humiliation, you're opportunistic and in denial of the levels of extent you will go to, in order to achieve fame, power or prestige. Superiority and self-delusion rule and you can be deceptive in order to get your way. If you make mistakes, you will do everything in your power to cover them up- even shifting blame or lying. Untrustworthy, calculated, jealous and envious, you are not yet connected to your source of talent and inspiration. You lack humility and are vindictive, obsessive, unhealthily relentless and psychotic in your pursuit for success. Essentially, narcissistic personality disorder is the main trait of an unhealthy and devolved type 3.

Type 4: The Individualist

Type 4s are individualists and romantics. They are dramatic, self-expressive, poetic and forward-thinking. Sensitivity is one of the greatest strengths and qualities of a type 4. If you're a type 4, you are very attuned to the realm of feelings and emotions. Inner currents and moods take precedence in your life, and you're deeply connected to the subconscious realms. You are unconditional love and universal compassion personified. You embody an advanced and highly evolved emotional frequency; when at your best, you're a natural healer, seer, psychic and counsellor- a listener and friend in need. You may be a spiritual guide or express yourself through poetry, music and art. Again, you're attuned to the realm of emotions and feelings, inner moods and subconscious insight. Your wisdom is intuitive and practical. You're both intelligent and deeply instinctual, so you're able to receive your guidance and knowledge from both reason, rationality & logic and the more ethereal and 'mystical' realms. You embody the vibration of the poet and philosopher.

You're a hopeless romantic. When channeled positively, this can lead to extraordinary creations in the artistic, academic, and creative fields. Your imagination is matched by no other! You possess the ability of tuning into universal archetypes and ideals to birth a new vibration for humanity. You're wise, perceptive, highly observant, and philosophical. You can be dramatic, but drama is also associated with the arts and creativity. Type 4s are suited to careers in the Arts, media, publishing and writing, performing arts, and professions such as becoming a musician, entertainer, performer or spoken word artist. Because of your unique sensitivity you also are best suited to working in literature, languages, teaching, astrology, the healing arts, spirituality, care and social/support, counselling, antiques and museums. You're intelligent but romantic, perceptive yet intuitive, wise and spiritually sightful, and logical but philosophical. Your sensitivity can be one of your greatest strengths as it leads to extraordinary insight, wisdom and awareness. You have a strong sense of self-identity.

One of your greatest strengths is the gift of equanimity, which means you have a unique gift for remaining calm and composed even in the most difficult situations. People see you as slightly reserved yet extremely intelligent and dependable-they know you can be trusted for your sound advice and unique perspectives. There's also something original and quirky about you, you stand out in a crowd. You're colorful and have a powerful spirit. Further, you have a deeply powerful and strong heart. You believe in harmony, unity consciousness, compromise and fairness, justice and social unity are important to you. In personal relationships you are warm, loving, caring and sincere. Nurturance, empathy, kindness and the ability to see the best in people and every situation are some of your greatest strengths. Your romantic nature means you have a deep love and respect for nature, which can make you very attractive. Seeing the world through a love of harmony, beauty and justice allows you to experience life with all of your senses. This equally enables you to provide for those you love in a way that opens them to connecting with their inner spirit. Nature, music, art, romance and introspection are integral to daily life.

When at your best you are positive and inspiring. You are able to remain optimistic and humble, even when the world treats you unfairly or unkindly. You can be extraordinarily selfless at times. A major positive aspect for type 4 is evolved creativity and ability to express universal human emotions through art, music, dance and poetry. You are highly compassionate, empathic, and idealistic with emotional depth and maturity, which saves you in many situations. Your authenticity, sincerity and empathy are qualities to be valued and cherished. The realm of universal truths, archetypes and insights into human nature and the meaning of life are areas not everyone can visit. But you access them quite effortlessly! Universe and metaphysics fascinate you too. If you choose a creative or artistic career path you will find your success stems from your capacity to connect to the spiritual and subconscious planes of being. Receiving sparks of insight and wisdom are common. You actually have a beautiful personality despite your low moods and struggles which we go into in 'Type 4 Shadow Traits.' Honesty, self-awareness, emotional intelligence and depth of soul are beautifully developed and balanced. You're kind, warm-hearted, generous and creatively gifted, and you can express yourself through a huge array of channels and outlets. Life is experienced with a sense of inspiration and artistic sight, vision and spiritual awareness.

At your best, you're able to learn from life's experience and reshape yourself, always changing, adapting and growing. Personal transformation and self-evolution are core components of a type 4. Your basic fear of a lack of personal identity can drive you to revolutionary transformation and shifts in growth. Your main life desire is to create a unique self-identity, and this allows you to inspire others through your own soul gifts and talents. You're primarily concerned with surrounding yourself with beauty, authentic connections, and emotional and spiritual bonds that have longevity. You're not interested in anything shallow or superficial. Depth, spirituality, soulmates and kindred spirits, community and romance favor strongly in your life. Your wish is to create and maintain certain moods and feelings from your environments and the universe, further channeling them into art and self-expression that can help or inspire others. Overall you are a very gifted individual who can see both the light and the dark and only feel compassion. The darkness is your friend and serves as a mirror or reflection to your soul and deep insight. You are blessed with the gifts of honesty and self-acceptance. When you're vibrating at your highest, self-denial and repressions don't even enter your conscious mind; you're as honest and pure in mind and spirit as they come.

You're fearless! You can see beauty in the "warts and all" and perfection within the imperfection. Finally, as a type 4 you are able to endure suffering and hardship with mighty strength. This strength is often hidden but it is there. You are a remarkable individual and transform your deepest wounds into a way to heal, uplift and inspire others.

Type 4 Shadow Traits

You're a very sensitive soul. There are quite a lot of issues and life challenges with type 4, but these all originate from the same source. This is your focus on the emotional aspect of life and self. Virtually all of your shadow traits stem from this one theme, your sensitivity and desire for maintaining a self-identity and sense of inspiration. You can be self-absorbed, hypersensitive, and reserved to the point of disconnection and separation. Isolation and loneliness are strong with a type 4. As a "hopeless romantic" and "lone wolf," you focus too much on the introspective worlds and therefore cut yourself off from society. This is where many imbalances and distortions arise. Becoming a victim, martyr or savior is common. Melancholy, low moods and depression often arise when you've been too attuned to mystical and ethereal realms. Philosophy, introspection and the subconscious are beautiful things, but everything in life requires balance. There is a natural darkness associated with this personality type; life involves light and dark- yang and yin, yet you are primarily attuned to your inner darkness.

Issues in self-worth, self-esteem, confidence and optimism can all arise when you've spent so long in solitude or silence. You become self-conscious, withdrawn, and down. You suffer unnecessarily and forget what it's like to laugh, be enthusiastic, and draw your energy from the sun and vital life force. Connections and platonic and romantic bonds can suffer, which further leads to a lack of inspiration in your path and creativity. The 'extraordinary' become ordinary when you close yourself off to others and the whole self. And, your entire identity and self-worth is tied into your amazing talents and unique perspectives! For someone who believes so strongly in harmony, beauty and balance, you can become surprisingly disconnected from your own inner harmony and balance and inner beauty. Thus, oversensitivity and melancholy are things you need to work on.

You also have a tendency to give into extreme forms of self-pity, self-doubt and vulnerability. Your vulnerabilities signify an unconscious feeling of self-righteousness and superiority- you know how powerful and pure you are (when at your best), but this deep love of beauty, romance and purity inevitably creates it's opposite; the duality and polar opposite. You then become self-righteous and arrogant or even more disconnected from others as a result. Ordinary ways of living are viewed as below or beneath you. You feel you're better than the ordinary and can *only* be attuned to the extraordinary. This isn't healthy, however. You therefore often struggle with practical and domestic affairs, mundane matters, finances and basic human connection. Type 4 is an incredibly divine and transcendental personality to have- you certainly know how to transcend the mundane and achieve elevated states of consciousness, creativity, imagination and self-awareness. Yet, again- life's meant to be balanced. Self-pity and self-indulgence are manifestations of this problem.

Romantic idealism, escapism, addictions and extreme bouts of separation are the other main aspects of your shadow self. You can be extremely selfless, yet this selflessness may not always serve you or your highest self; envy, severe melancholy and closing your heart to others or those closest to you occur. You strongly desire a secure self-identity and social persona. Your ability to feel safe, secure and comforted arise from having a persona others can relate to, connection is essential for your health and well-being. It is the root of reality for you. Yet, you frequently feel socially awkward. You feel like you don't belong and don't fit in. *Do you create this yourself?* The answer is yes; you desire so desperately to maintain a strong self-identity that you often have a very difficult time fitting in. You are the misfit or oddball of society. This isn't a bad thing when channeled positively through art, creativity and inspiration, but can be the source of your downfall and most of the major challenges you face in life. The best way to overcome this is to learn how to receive pleasure and emotional comfort from the daily rituals and routines of life. *Grounding* is important for you.

Your key is to understand that you can be different, unique and divinely inspired *while* remaining connected to your roots, to the physical world and your society or community. Being different and special should be a blessing, not a curse! It's often like you have a secret love story with feeling misunderstood (your archetype is the "hopeless romantic") so work on this. Your self-esteem will increase, and you'll begin to feel as one part of a greater whole, which is your main life's desire. Don't shoot yourself in the foot, in other words. Fantasy is strong too. Fantasy can lead to illusions, self-delusion, depression and disconnection from reality. You can meditate on social grace and charm, willpower, inner strength, and emotional tranquility to help with this. Also, the fire element is something you need to work on increasing to achieve more balance and abundance in life. Be careful of the victim-martyr-savior complex. We go into self-development techniques later.

Type 4s: Rumi, Tchaikovsky, Frederic Chopin, Virginia Woolf, Anne Frank, Tennessee Williams, Bob Dylan, Prince, Billie Holiday, Alanis Morrisette, and Amy Winehouse.

Levels of Development

Healthy Levels: -

1. **When at your Best**: You are profoundly artistic and imaginatively gifted and creative. You have a direct link to the divine, subconscious and transcendental realms, and universal archetypes and insights into consciousness. You are on a path of self-mastery, transformation and personal growth- life involves frequent renewal & rebirth and chances for integration of life cycles (lessons). You're inspiring and inspired!

2. **Slightly below your best**: You're introspective, self-aware, talented and creative. You believe in a higher power and access it on a regular basis. You're sensitive

and intuitive, gentle and compassionate and use these gifts to create things that you believe will inspire or heal others. You live life in flow and are generally content.

3. **Nearly there**: You're true to yourself, personal and relatable. People see you as an individual and recognize you for your unique insights and perspectives on life. Honest, emotionally intelligent, tactful and moral, the way you present yourself is positive and authentic. You're vulnerable and sometimes show your low moods and depressive tendencies, but know how to put on a smile and bounce back. You've chosen to commit to a positive mindset and inspiring lifestyle.

Average levels: -

4. **On the Path**: You've adopted a romantic, philosophical and artistic outlook on life, and you're committed to creating beauty around you. You still have your follies, you struggle with melancholy and depression/low moods from time to time, and you can be quite vulnerable. But you are emotionally strong and self-aware. Passionate feelings, fantasy and the imagination take precedence in your life.

5. **Learning, still in the Shadow stage**: Your reality is heightened through fantasy and the make-believe. You're deeply in touch with your feelings, positive and negative, and are extremely sensitive. You take things personally and can be introverted, moody and withdrawn sometimes. You're hypersensitive however possess wisdom and intuitive inner guidance into your own behavior and human nature as a whole. You enjoy solitude and feel the need to protect yourself often.

6. **Devolved**: You live life in mild fear and depression. You're sensitive and aware- you certainly have wisdom and a strong need for self-identity, yet you don't know how to express this properly. Fantasy, extreme sensuality, disconnection and feeling different from everyone are common. Self-pity, self-indulgence and envy often leave you feeling scared to be your true self, and you still feel like you will be judged or even persecuted for shining in your truest light. You're not yet comfortable in your own body and self and tend to be overly impractical.

Unhealthy levels

You're depressed, alienated, blocked and emotionally repressed. You frequently feel shame, fear and dissatisfaction with yourself and life. Additions are strong and you are very impractical, disconnected from both your body and the world around. Self-pity, self-indulgence, delusions and denial are strong while you shift responsibility and blame to others. There is a small aspect of divinity and inspiration in your life, however it is a glimpse of your future self. You suffer daily and get lost in despair and melancholy- self-destruction and hopelessness having taken precedence over your artistic and intuitive gifts. Emotional breakdown, suicidal feelings, extreme isolation and social anxiety are regular occurrences. You can see light, but it is a distant dream...

Type 5: The Investigator

Type 5s are also known as Investigators or Observers. They are innovative, intelligent, and original thinkers. 5s excel in all matters of logic, reason and problem-solving. You thrive in scholarly, academic and creative pursuits and are a knowledge seeker. Your observation skills are on a whole new level, life is one elongated sensory experience for you; you're always taking note of your surroundings and the things you perceive. Generally, upbeat and positive, optimism is drawn from your ability to discover hidden truths and unseen meanings or motives. You possess the unique ability of becoming emotionally detached too- and this makes you deeply analytical and logical in your conclusions. But you also possess intuition. You're connected to your inner light and use it as a guide throughout life. This gift can make you incredibly relatable. You're intellectual, wise, talented and witty, able to use your wit and mind to connect with others. You do have a tendency to be quiet and sullen or withdrawn, but when this occurs consciously (mindfully) it's because you're deep in thought and introspection. This increases your wisdom.

This is a very self-sufficient personality type. Self-autonomy and creating your own blessings and abundance in life are important to you. Positively this enables you to be a proud individual who is ambitious, focused, and committed to your talents and professional or monetary pursuits. If you choose to have a family it also makes you a wonderful parent and caregiver, you love presenting yourself as a practical and responsible adult and have fair amounts of natural nurturance and instincts. Primarily, however, you are focused on your intellectual and scholarly pursuits in life which further have the potential to translate into a successful career. Self-reliance, personal authority and power define you. Slacking or getting lost in laziness or lethargy is seldom seen with a type 5 (although you do need to be mindful of extremes, as we explore in your

Shadow Traits). Creatively and artistically gifted, many 5s make a name for themselves in some artistic or imaginative field. Your level of perceptiveness isn't just limited to the academic fields. At a higher emotional frequency, you are capable of extraordinary levels of emotional intelligence and empathy, with empathy being the ability to know what it feels like to be in another's shoes; feeling deeply. This isn't birthed through a spiritual or emotional connection as it is with empaths, for example, but your empathy occurs through the mental planes. You understand things on a deep level, and this opens up channels to aspects of psychic or seer-like connection. You can see inside another thus getting to the root of buried truths or insecurities, problems or talents, thoughts and feelings. Being so mentally and cerebrally gifted means you are naturally clairvoyant, however how much so will all depend on how much you work on these gifts.

So, your best qualities lie in the realms of intellect, logic, reason, self-reliance and self-autonomy, and non-attachment leading to advanced observation. Your capacity for non-attachment equally helps when working on yourself, so in aspects of self-development. You can overcome any potential negative or shadow personality traits through tapping into your innate gifts, the ability to detach and observe, see reason and understand on a deeper level, free form judgement. Your challenge can lead to your self-evolution as well which is becoming more connected with your feelings. When at your best, you're both psychologically gifted and mentally perceptive, and sensitive and emotionally in tune. Feeling leads to greater intuitive abilities and a more developed instinct. Emotions and feelings are a core part to your whole personality and it's important that you seek to develop these. Due to the fact that you love accumulating knowledge you will most likely become an expert in your field. This personality type symbolizes the highest possible academic achievement. Material wealth and success is available too once you've started to become recognized in your field and secure within your talents and gifts.

Positive harmonious relationships serve as a mirror for you, but- again- these do need some work. You're intense, innovative, communicative and constantly seeking wisdom, higher ideals and truths, and abstract or philosophical concepts. You may also be interested in metaphysics. Your cerebral gifts allow you to see things others might miss, whether it's about the cosmos, science, philosophy, technology or spirituality- you wish to know all there is to know. And, this manifests as being an amazing networker and social butterfly, or asset in a team, organization or party. You're happy to share pearls of wisdom and inform or inspire others through your knowledge reserves. You can be seen as a living library later in life, certainly from your 30s or mid to late twenties if you've applied yourself. You're always searching, always asking questions and always pursuing deeper meanings. Imaginative gifts are integral to type 5s. One other thing that is a strength (when expressed positively and not steered towards the shadow self/personality) is your dislike and strong aversion to opinions. You don't do well with other people's opinions, judgments or dogma- but thrive in universal truths, perspectives and debate. Open-mindedness allows you to connect to people from all walks of life, and further helps lead to your success.

Because of your love of depth, you can find beauty in a flower, lake or stream, or leaf. Nature fascinates you and aids in your scholarly and imaginative pursuits. You might decide to become a quantum physicist or researcher into the holographic and interconnected nature of reality. Truth to you is a subjective experience yet you're wise enough to combine intuitive with logic & reason to create your own conclusions. Furthermore, this helps you to establish a firm set of morals and ethics, principles to live by. As a type 5, you absorb sensory data and information from the world to make sense of experiences, and to create your own beliefs and ideologies. Once you've had enough experiences you transform these into principles and set guidelines to live by, with each belief adopted becomes a foundation for further learning and knowledge acquisition. Spending a lot of time observing and contemplating is common. You find joy and contentment in listening to the sounds of wind, water or birds, people watching and observing the simple tranquility of nature or children playing. Human relationships, exchanges, and interactions inspire you as well. You're genuinely interested in human nature, the meaning of life and the universe- life has a certain magic to it when you're operating at your best. You're able to immerse yourself in an observation and experience and then internalize the knowledge before sharing it externally.

Imaginative, innovative, largely independent and curious, you are a blessing in the world once you step into your true power and self-alignment. Sparks of insight come to you through inquisitiveness. Your attention is often drawn to the bizarre, occult, secret, unseen, supernatural, mystical or unusual, anything "overlooked" and "undervalued;" and investigating unknown territory allows you to gain the self-esteem and confidence necessary to follow your dreams and achieve success. This is where your pearls of wisdom are found. You're a gem when attuned to your inner knowing, personal confidence and wise power. You possess well-developed self-esteem and personal authority later in life. Alert, insightful, curious, intelligent and inventive, this is the life path associated with inventors, scientists, teachers of quantum physics or mysticism, philosophers, artists, poets, painters, musicians, and evolutionaries. Great advancements in technology, science and spirituality can come about when you set your mind on something. At your best, you are a problem-solver who can work with very complex ideas and details. You're a pioneer- a visionary and changemaker and are gifted with unique sight and perceptive skills. Being "ahead of the times" and "ahead of your time" are associated with type 5.

You can use your basic fear and primary desire to stay inspired throughout the course of your life. Your basic fear is of being useless or incapable while your main desire is to be recognized (for your knowledge and level of expertise), capable and competent. Key motivations include possessing knowledge, understanding others, the world and your environment, and figuring things out to uncover deeper or hidden truths. Spiritual seekers are associated with type 5 just as much as inventors and innovators in science, academia and technology are.

Type 5 Shadow Traits

Amongst all your positives you do have some shadow traits. Secrecy and fear of not being seen as capable or reliable are arguably your greatest shadow qualities. You have a tendency to become too detached, isolated and secretive, also being cut off from your feelings. As this personality type is associated with thinking, cerebral qualities and the mind, you neglect your emotions and internal needs. There is a large focus on the external- outside ideas, concepts, perspectives and philosophies, yet this disconnects you from the inner world. The inner worlds are equally important, they relate to moods, emotions, inner sensations, sexuality, desires, emotional needs and wants, and everything connected to the maternal, emotional and spiritual. Type 5s are emotionally detached and spiritually disconnected when at their worst. It can be very difficult for you to open up and express your feelings, share your emotions and desires, and generally connect with others in a transparent and vulnerable way.

A lack of vulnerability, openness and emotional trust are some of your worst traits. Being so inquisitive and intelligent creates many opportunities. It opens channels on a variety of levels. But, it disallows you from experiencing the joys and pleasures of human connection, sensual play and expression, and instinctual feeling and bonding. In other words, showing and sharing affection, love, warmth, and intimacy (and receiving these things). It also signifies that you get stuck in your mind often, resulting in severe overthinking and disconnection from your body and the world around. Many type 5s have issues in sexual intimacy and mature bonding-deeper and long-lasting connections. Isolation is a major problem throughout life. You cut yourself off from opportunities, new experiences, and play, which equally means you cut yourself off from being part of a community or team working towards a common goal. The other end of the spectrum is the internal issues that can arise when you spend so much time in isolation, and out of tune with your feelings and bodily needs. Promiscuity and crude attitudes towards sex and intimacy can take over, or you can simply be deeply confused and unable to express your feelings and urges. Unhealthy attitudes and behaviors towards both sexual and platonic connections can therefore be adopted.

Secrecy is another main flaw to this personality type, which only leads further to the distortions in your emotional body. Further, sometimes when you're being quiet and introspective in a positive way, i.e. in genuine and healthy contemplation or mindful observation, people can mistake your quietness for arrogance or conceit. There is a lot of misjudgment and misperception associated with type 5. This, of course, further leads to extreme self-isolation; it's a brutal cycle, but one all personality types must go through to find balance and wholeness within (with each Enneatype having a different cycle to transcend). For you it is about alchemizing your sensitivity and inquisitiveness into something others can relate to. Self-compassion and cultivating self-awareness will help. If people mistake your silence or reservations for arrogance, this creates a disconnect from the wisdom you have to share- and therefore your confidence and self-esteem. If you can learn to develop healthy boundaries and work on the energy or image you project, you will have better luck at being seen for the intelligent and slightly introverted character that you are. In addition, you can be very intense, highly strung and eccentric. Be careful of nihilism too, nihilism being the belief that life is meaningless. Your perpetual seeking of knowledge means you may adopt so many beliefs and theories that you create the mindset that life is itself meaningless! There is a case of "too much" leading to "nothing," everything and nothing existing simultaneously; you reject all religious and moral principles because you understand how all can be true.

This is both a curse and blessing. On the one hand, you're deeply intelligent, philosophical, wise and intuitive. You see how all theories and discoveries into the meaning of life are possible. But, this in itself leads you to reject them all. This makes you unconsciously reject parts of yourself but falling into the emptiness and nothingness; the "darkness" (as opposed to the everything and "lightness"). Your relentless pursuit of knowledge also leads to considerable insecurity. Your primary fear in life is being seen as incompetent, incapable and useless but you set extremely high standards for yourself. You tend to judge yourself unconsciously without realizing the expectations you create. It's a bit like a 'self-perpetuating prophecy,' you unconsciously set yourself up for disappointment. You should learn that you are enough, and that you can be an expert in your field without punishing yourself (such as by falling into isolation or disconnection). Finally, issues are frequently pushed under the rug. Instead of dealing with issues hands-on, you work on making yourself more competent or knowledgeable. This may be problems in finances, work, relationships, career or health, whatever it is you deny it and resort to energizing (improving) the same area you always do. This helps with your mind and wisdom, once again, but keeps the same cycles on repeat. Anxiety, practical problems, self-care and the inability to form close personal relationships are all shadow aspects associated with the type 5 personality.

Overall, secrecy and isolation can be your greatest downfalls. Opening your heart to the beauty of connection and the magic of co-creation; the endless possibilities associated with intimacy and sharing- will transform your life in many wonderful ways. Social isolation can be combated with improving confidence, friendships, and internal feelings.

Type 5s: Siddartha Guatama Buddha, Albert Einstein, John Nash, Stephen Hawking, Vincent van Gogh, Emily Dickinson, Friedrich Nietzsche, James Joyce, Stephen King, Eckhart Tolle, Kurt Cobain, Bill Gates, Mark Zuckerberg, and Julian Assange.

Levels of Development

Healthy Levels: -

1. **When at your Best**: You're a visionary and a changemaker, someone who uses their deeply developed wisdom, beliefs & perspectives into the meaning of life, the universe, and human nature to help others. You are able to share and connect with others easily and understand things on a deep level. You're intuitive, self-expressive, wise and open-minded with a unique perspective on the world.

2. **Slightly below your best**: You're highly observant, intuitive and intelligent. You're open-minded and believe in the power of silent observation, introspection and contemplation. You've started making pioneering discoveries and are well on your way to be a shining example and changemaker. You possess keen insights into

many things including yourself, the self and psyche, and the cosmos/universe.

3. **Nearly there**: You're mentally alert, curious and inquisitive. You're able to perceive things others can't and often get to the root of hidden truths, meanings and unseen knowledge. You're gifted with foresight, intuition and powerful observation skills, yet you still have an issue with relating to others completely authentically. Intimacy and personal relationships suffer (slightly) on your pursuit of wisdom.

All of the 3 top levels include innovation, inventiveness and skillful mastery. Independence, originality, and expertise define you.

Average levels: -

4. **On the Path**: You've started to conceptualize things and fine-tune your understanding of the world, and your own observation skills. You're wise, perceptive and extremely curious, already showing signs of inventiveness and originality. You are, however, plagued by your fears and have some blocks to work through. Close relationships suffer and you're prone to

isolation. In saying this, you know who you are and are in the processing of acquiring wisdom, knowledge and resources to achieve self-realization.

5. **Learning, still in the Shadow stage**: The imagination and fantasy worlds take precedence. You're detached emotionally and not in tune with your feelings, but you are intellectual and open-minded to learning and wisdom acquisition. Ideas can be complex, and insight muddled- you're not yet sure of who you are or what you're destined to create or achieve in this lifetime. Visions and ideals replace reality while mystery, the occult, esotericism and everything dark and unseen are more interesting to you than roots, relationships, and practical affairs.

6. **Devolved**: You love learning but are cynical, argumentative, judgmental and radical in your views. You're antagonistic, nihilistic, emotionally detached and sometimes a bit of a "know-it-all." If someone questions your inner world or vision you treat them like an enemy, or an idiot! You've got a lot to learn but your intelligence and cerebral skills are shining through.

Isolated, reclusive, secretive and undisciplined, life is a bit of a dream and haze. You're eccentric, nihilistic, unstable and impractical- you can be away with the fairies while adopting beliefs not rooted in reality nor wisdom. Social attachments are rejected, and you don't want to learn from elders or wise teachers. Nightmares, insomnia, depression and irrational fears can take hold. You also become obsessed yet frightened by your ideas, mental distortions, phobias, and psychotic episodes can take over. Also, explosive anger or emotional breakdowns can be common and there are aspects of schizophrenia. There's a rejection of self, nutrition, hygiene and self-care too.

Type 6: The Loyalist

Type 6's are known as 'Loyalists.' They are responsible, committed, loyal and trustworthy. These people are attentive to people's problems, needs and concerns. They're intuitive, caring, sincere and community or teamwork oriented. Similar to type 2, relationships are an integral part of a type 6s life and path. Type 6s often enjoy long-lasting and mutually respecting relationships and can be wonderfully devoted in both love and platonic partnerships. Self-awareness is a gift- as a type 6 you are able to be in the know of what's going on around you. You're receptive, nurturing, supportive and intuitive to the needs of others. This is a very feminine personality type, so regardless of your sexual orientation or gender, you will find yourself wanting to take on a nurturing and providing role throughout life. You're protective, blessed with intuition and wisdom, and instinctual. You're also gifted mentally. Cerebral and psychological abilities are strong and developed, you can balance intuition and feeling with perceptiveness and logic, reason and analysis. Intellectual and open-minded, as a loyalist you can succeed in a number of professions or paths.

You are actually a brave and devoted individual with lots of inner fire. Courage is one of your greatest, yet often hidden, assets. Your passion and devotion to cause enables you to be a shining light and rock for others in time of need. It also allows you to wade your way into a crowd to defend the underdog, or burst into a situation with dignity and poise while exerting your personal power and force. You're compassionate and selfless but strong and connected to your truth. Courage and fiery passion help you throughout life from at home and within the family to in social situations. Self-leadership defines you. You're fearless and altruistic, a natural humanitarian and believer in social justice, fairness and cooperation. Type 6s are symbolic of humanitarian aid workers who travel to distant lands or dangerous locations to help others. They're also symbolic of healers, caregivers, support workers, nurses, therapists, counsellors and charity workers, welfare givers and the selfless souls who dedicate significant portions of time to vulnerable children, adults and animals. Selfless and altruistic, type 6s are compassion and care embodied. Because you're a natural leader and assertive, and gentle and benevolent simultaneously, you may find yourself drawn to being a leader and boss or follower and team player equally. You can thrive in a position of leadership and authority just as you would be happy being employed and merging into the background.

You possess healthy boundaries and wisdom to accompany. You make a wonderful friend, lover and team-player, and often focus on and direct your energy towards community projects and groupwork. You can thrive in a crisis and possess a unique courage and strength which comes with an innate loyalty to self and others. You are attentive, fearless and loyal- people trust you and know they can count on you for your honest, but tactful advice and guidance. Further, you seek out security and stability in all you do, and this allows you to form connections with longevity. Business, marriage, love and family bonds, romance and platonic friendships are all valued to you and areas you can achieve the most happiness in life. Commitment isn't something you're shy of! You're also the type of person to 'go down with the ship' and do everything in your power to make a relationship or project work. There's little room for quitting with you. You're reliable, hardworking, dedicated and responsible. You're a force to be reckoned with, in fact, in your own subtly powerful and non-intrusive way. People sense your sincerity and kindness and want to be your friend. You're able to foresee problems with incredible wisdom and intuitive insight too. Your loyalty opens pathways towards the growth and nurturance of projects, places and relationships that extent beyond the norm. In other words, there are certain lines you can transcend because of your staging-power and foresight.

The beautiful thing about a 6's mind is that they are aware of their insecurities and vulnerabilities. There's something incredibly beautiful about a balanced, open and vulnerable type 6. Even when they are balanced, they still show signs of minor anxiety and insecurity- and this makes them cherished and adored by those who know them. As a type 6, you are so attentive and caring, nurturing and proactive it is in your nature to worry. Anxiety, worry and emotional sensitivity are intrinsic to your core nature, thus even when you are at your best you will still display these traits. Imagine a fiercely protective, yet kind and compassionate mother. This is the energy of type 6. You are fiercely passionate, devoted and protective; you're kind, altruistic, intuitive and selfless when you need to be. There are certain things that one can't escape from when they take on a certain role. Your vulnerabilities and insecurities inspire you to become the best version of yourself you can be. They inspire you to be the nurturer and loving friends, partner or colleague- they push you towards self-mastery at a level that is sustainable for you. You realize that there is perfection in imperfections, and you see it as perfect. This makes you have a beautiful mind, spirit and soul.

Due to your strength, fierce protectiveness, and brave loyalty you may engage in conscious rebellion. This can manifest through your ideas, beliefs adopted, personal practices, career path, or protests and active rebellion. You're a visionary and changemaker however prefer to put your energy into close relationships and bonds. Netherthless, you still have a strong aspect of a conscious rebellitor and visionary. You're loyal to the core and believe that all power and authority should be questioned. You're inquisitive, curious, empathic and intelligent. Happy to challenge the status quo, you see questions and things society has labeled as "conspiracies" as an opportunity for self-evolution and consciousness expansion. Alternative viewpoints and realities aren't negative to you- they are portals into learning and self-discovery. There's a revolutionary, anti-authoritarian and idealistic aspect about your character. You can fight for your beliefs and others (including the vulnerable, animals and the planet!) more fiercely than you will sometimes stand up for yourself. You're okay with this, as- again- it draws from your inner strength and adds to your beautiful qualities of caring and nurturance. Positively, you will defend your family, soulmate or loved ones to the final breath when you have no more energy to fight for what is right and just.

Type 6s make excellent children's teachers, caregivers, creative teachers and counsellors and therapists. With 6 being a feminine number you also possess an element of psychic ability. Dreams, the occult, spiritual and psychic development, clairvoyance, astrology and metaphysics, tarot and divination all fascinate you, so these are possible career paths and vocations. At your best you are self-reliant, internally stable, responsible and devoted. Commitment and loyalty come naturally to you and it is easy for you to open up emotionally, mentally/psychologically, physically and spiritually to others. You're a champion for the underdog and people in need of learning, support, or guidance, and your basic desire of security inspires you to connect to your strengths (and not your shadow). You love to laugh, connect and engage in family and community ties and genuinely desire support, love and affection.

Type 6 Shadow Traits

Type 6s are anxious, suspicious and very worrisome. Due to your need for security and connection you may sometimes become anxious and suspicious, and you tend to dwell on the negative. You're cautious of others and give in to procrastination quite regularly. Indecisiveness can take over your life at times, in fact. Anxiety and indecisiveness stems from your caring and nurturing, from your desire to be a support system in people's lives. One thing you lack in is self-care and taking time for yourself, and this leads to your negative attributes. In comparison, your shadow personality traits aren't that bad and are generally things everyone suffers with from time to time. But, without check and conscious awareness you can fall into extremes. And this is where more severe health problems arise.

So, mainly you need to work on stress and anxiety from taking on too much. Linked to this is defensiveness, you can become surprisingly defensive and take things personally. You are so wrapped up in intimate connections and relationships that you begin to lose your sense of self. At your worst, boundaries are an issue (although this is something you are usually quite good with, when centered and strong within). Weak boundaries lead to you feeling victimized, targeted, or used and offended when there was no offense or harmful intentions. Self-delusion isn't a major issue for you, but giving into too much pessimistic thinking and "victim consciousness" can make you see things that aren't there. Stresses and anxiety are a common occurrence and taking things personally or to heart makes you question yourself, resulting in diminished self-esteem and personal confidence. Insecurities can be strong with a type 6. Self-doubt and suspicions can be eased with meditation, nature therapy, and self-healing. Also, you believe that you don't possess the internal resources necessary to succeed or handle life's challenges. You thus increasingly rely on outside beliefs, friendships & partnerships, structures, and support systems for your strength. This inevitably leads to more worry, anxiety and reduced confidence. Responsibility and reliability are some of your weaknesses when you're less evolved.

Due to your need for social security, trust can be a major problem for you. It can be hard for you to open up and trust others completely, you always hold a bit of yourself back at first or make excuses to prevent a connection from blossoming. This does heal over time, and depending on your personal past and any wounds or traumatic experiences you may have suffered the extent of this will vary. In general, you are trustworthy yet find it difficult to trust others. Intuition and inner guidance aid greatly with this. The key to know with this personality type is that 6s are both weak and strong, fearful and brave, distrusting and trusting, indecisive and courageous…. Although it's not a number of dualities, there are many opposing forces embodied. One minute you may be brave and fearless and the next you will be overcome with insecurity and meekness. In one moment, you feel empowered and have a fierce sense of protectiveness about you- the next, you will be stuck in silence and shyness. Other 'dualities' you often struggle with or simply experience are: defending and provoking, believing and doubting, bullying and being bullied/weakness, aggression and passivity, thinking and feeling, being a team player and going solo, gentleness and over-assertion, and being cooperative and being the rebel!

All of these are birthed from your need of security and stability. If you don't feel cherished, loved, supported, seen, heard, understood, secure or grounded you can become anything and everything, giving into a range of opposites. Craving connection and feeling safe within your environments can have the opposite effect if you're not feeling safe and secure within. There is a blessing in this personality type, however; as mentioned earlier an inherent part of your core nature is being aware of the power of insecurity, anxiety, and imperfection. You actually manage to find serenity and peace in the uncertainty and duality. Self-acceptance is key to your happiness, health and success. So, confidence, self-judgement and overthinking are the main struggles throughout life. The other main shadow aspects are being rebellious and defiant. When vibrating at your lowest frequency, you may get involved in unlawful protests or be a rebel. Your primary fear is the fear of abandonment and being left without love and support, so *disconnection* holistically. You need to feel part of a community or social, family and/or friendship circle. When expressed negatively this makes you play out your insecurities, therefore one thing you need to be mindful of is projection. Instead of mirroring beautiful and positive qualities to others, you *project* the insecurities and fears within.

In all honesty, all the Enneatypes can look to the Shadow Traits of a type 6, as these are the fundamentals of wound and trauma healing. They're patterns of behavior and thinking we all must transcend and outgrow on our journey into adulthood. However, for you as type 6 they are more apparent and possible your only flaws and follies. Your primary vibration is one of a higher, empathic, and unconditionally loving energy. You're naturally capable of authentic and deep bonds and emotional connection (again, something many people have to work on based on specific character/personality traits).

Type 6s: Krishnamurti, Sigmund Freud, Robert F. Kennedy, Malcolm X, George Bush, Princess Diana of Wales, Prince Harry, J.R.R. Tolkien, Eminem, Marilyn Monroe, and Woody Allen.

Levels of Development

Healthy Levels: -

1. **When at your Best**: You're incredibly trusting, devoted, loyal and self-affirming. Relationships serve as a mirror and reflection into your soul, self, psyche, and greatest desires and passions. You're independent and cooperative simultaneously, thriving in team and group situations and being a vital part of a community, social network, or circle. People look to you for your courage, wisdom, kindness and authenticity; however, you choose to express it personally. You're

artistically and imaginatively gifted with a unique creativity.

2. **Slightly below your best**: You're brave, devoted, passionate and positive thinking. You possess an optimistic outlook on life and exhibit self-leadership, understanding and empathy. You're altruistic and endearing, loveable and affectionate, a valued member of your community or family. You may not be a bold and inspiring charismatic leader, but you are highly cherished through the bonds you've formed.

3. **Nearly there**: You're committed and dedicated to others and a select number of movements. Projects and causes that require your love and help are valued by you, and others see you for your gifts. Responsibility, reliability and trustworthiness define you, and you're known for your hard-working and self-sacrificing nature. You can be overly self-sacrificing at times, giving into your sensitivities and lack of self-care, however. You possess a cooperative spirit.

Average levels: -

4. **On the Path**: You've begun investing your time and resources into movements, people and projects that move you. You're a

community builder, passionate, committed and devoted to a cause. Your empathy, compassion and cooperative spirit are powerful and you're an excellent organizer; you're reliable, hard-working and trustworthy. You seek security but still give into self-doubt and insecurity, anxiety and projection from time to time.

5. **Learning, still in the Shadow stage**: You're reactive and defensive, passive aggressive and procrastinating. You've foreseen your goals and dreams and possess a clear vision, yet you're still dealing with stuff internally. You can be pessimistic and small-minded while giving into anxiety, but, you're aware of your strengths and are capable of moments of real depth, beauty & intimacy.

6. **Devolved**: You anticipate problems quite frequently and have a negative mindset. You can be sarcastic, highly reactive and defensive, and insecure whilst unconsciously projecting onto others. You've yet to develop and integrate your emotional openness, intelligence and vulnerability, therefore others see you as closed. Blaming others and shifting responsibility are common. Also, you're suspicious, plagued by fears and illusions, authoritarian and self-doubting. Your empathy, love and desires for affection

are hidden and only come out in glimmers (although they are apparent).

Unhealthy levels

The unhealthiest levels of type 6 are portrayed by characteristics of panicking, volatility, defenselessness, belittlement, emotional or physical violence, and extreme anxiety and irrational fears. You seek out authority figures and someone to 'save' you, yet simultaneously fear authority and feel persecuted and/or victimized. Irrational behavior is frequent, and you act out, like a teenager would; you can be hysterical, melodramatic, disconnected from reality and escapist. Drugs and addictions are likely, paranoia can take over, and diet, health and nutrition suffer.

Type 7: The Enthusiast

Type 7s are 'Enthusiasts,' spontaneous and fun-loving individuals. These are the people who seem restless, full of energy, and always on the go. They are full of life force and vitality, passion and a sense of excitement- their energy can be contagious and highly inspiring. Type 7s are forward thinkers, progressive and all about action, movement and motion. They possess profound mental skills and abilities and are deeply cerebral in nature. If you are a type 7, you are high spirited, extroverted and extremely sociable. You enjoy staying busy and have an optimistic, upbeat and positive spirit, more so than any of the other Enneatypes, in fact. Travel, adventure and intellectual pursuits and interests are some of your favorite activities and pastimes. Type 7's can be deeply inspirational and bring an optimism and unique energy to those around them. You like to keep your options open and are generally not too concerned with other people's opinions or perceptions of you. You're self-autonomous and fun-loving and when you've learned how to balance your adventure-seeking, free-spirited nature with some grounding and security, or commitment, you can achieve a lot in life! At your best you are blessed with the gift of sobriety, inner happiness and contentment, and balance. Presence is where you draw your inner strength when more evolved, balanced and mature.

You're busy, adaptable, open-minded and spontaneous. Versatility is one of your greatest gifts and this allows you to connect and converse with people from all walks of life. You're cultured and energetic, philosophical and open to expanding your horizons. You almost bounce into a room or environment, there is an aura of warmth, stardom and color around you; you project confidence and self-esteem. You're playful too. This personality type is suited to a creative or arts teacher, digital nomad, freelancer, tour guide or any field in the Arts, media, tourism and hospitality. Wanderlust defines you; your spirit is free, and you like to make many connections in life. Children inspire you as well- you bounce off of their energy and ideas, enjoying the zest and passion they provide. Because of your extroverted nature, you don't do too well spending lots of time alone. Positively this makes you an excellent party or wedding planner, host/hostess, manager, social organizer or leader, boss and entrepreneur. Ideas and wisdom flows to you effortlessly when you feel appreciated and heard. Thus, you can work well as part of a team or going solo, but you do require social bonds and a feeling of 'community spirit.'

Type 7s are associated with kindred spirits and alternative lifestyles. You may leave your traditional job and expand your skills online, such as by becoming a freelance writer, editor, illustrator, graphic designer, or the like. Working from your laptop or anywhere in the world is suited to you and it means you can feed your adventurous and travel-loving spirit. You're multi-talented, for the most part and if you apply yourself, and constantly seek new and exciting experiences. Your character is joyous, positive, appreciative and independent. Type 7 is labelled the 'Enthusiast' as you are upbeat and optimistic in all you do. Your attention-span can be short (as we explore in your Shadow Traits) but overall this leads you to try and experience many things, adopt many belief systems and viewpoints, and be a colorful and open-minded individual. Bold and courageous are two key words to describe you. You take on the world with a 'can do attitude;' you're determined and level-headed, and you enjoy speaking your truth and sharing your ideas, feelings and beliefs. Affectionate, loving, playful and intelligent, you are deeply self-expressive. To add, being so anti-oppression and anti-suppression allows you to expand and broaden your horizons… you're deeply against being restricted, suppressed or oppressed at all- limitations frighten you and make you feel trapped. And this motivates you to step into self-authority, self-leadership and inner strength. You draw your courage and confidence from the thought of being oppressed or restricted in any way, which can be very positive and encouraging.

You're a natural problem-solver and not afraid of a challenge. You're curious, inquisitive, perceptive and vivacious... charismatic, brave, effervescent and cheerfully determined. Many people automatically see you as so playful and free-spirited that they assume you are impractical or disconnected from reality. Yet, behind your cheerful and high energized exterior you possess powerful and subtle ambition, a genuine desire to succeed and better yourself.

Learning, higher education, study and philosophy, culture and travel, and financial and professional success all inspire you. You can be very responsible and practical when you want to be. Also, you tend to be engaged in many projects and passion pursuits simultaneously which opens pathways to prosperity and new opportunities. You are a lucky soul! Emotionally affectionate, spiritually open, and physically and practical balanced, you do tend to be more connected to the mental and intellectual planes, however. You are generally balanced but do prefer mental and intellectual connections, as this is where your wisdom, insight and inspiration comes from. You're innovative. You're not as inventive and academic as a type 5, but you are widely read and highly verbal- and this makes you appear intelligent. Adaptability and flexibility of thoughts and the mind is one of your most developed strengths.

You're also a pleasure seeker, creative innovation is where you thrive and an out of balance 7 will show signs of quite clearly not being themselves. Creativity is a source of joy and satisfaction for you. If you've stopped being creative, expressing yourself imaginatively and artistically, and stopped playing (allowing your inner child to be free etc.) then you know something is wrong, something needs to be healed. On a positive, you have an agile and quick-witted mind. You're an extremely fast learner and are gifted with an exceptional memory. Type 7s can remember things from and through every stage of life, and even the details most people overlook; you absorb information effortlessly and use this to form connections. Facts and figures, languages, emotional experiences and memories- you've got your mind sussed. Manual skills are a strong point to you as well and you tend to have evolved mind-body coordination. Energetic, skillful and determined, you like learning things and gathering a range of skills to showcase and make use of. A grounded type 7 is productive, hard-working and ambitious, not afraid to get their hands dirty and immerse themselves completely in the task at hand. You possess abundant vitality and participate fully in your life; you don't take the backseat. You're naturally cheerful, good-humored, funny and open to laughter and connection while being able to show your emotions and affections positively to those you love. Warm-hearted, funny, friendly, outgoing, kind, and magnanimous are other keywords to describe you.

Your primary desire in life is to be satisfied, happy and content. Your basic fear is being deprived, limited, oppressed/suppressed or restricted. Both your drive & desire and fear can lead you to going after your dreams and attaining self-realization. You don't like to take yourself too seriously but do commit to self-development and inner balance and harmony. Inner balance and harmony are very important to you and you recognize that they help lead to your joy and prosperity. You're motivated by freedom and individual liberty, by social and community ties and activities, and by wish fulfillment. Your energy and optimism can be infectious, so it is significant to work on your shadow traits and tendencies to find true happiness in life; your gift to the world is the gift of pure pleasure, freedom, and being an example of living a joyous existence.

Type 7 Shadow Traits

Type 7 can be easily distracted, restless and unfocused. Your worst personality traits are having too many eggs in too many baskets, and then watching the eggs shatter and not really caring! You're scattered, uncommitted, and self-absorbed-you go through life as if you are a wanderer, not really paying a second mind to the people, projects or relationships you've begun and then let go of along the way. This is a very frivolous personality type to have. You might start things without finishing them and then let go as if they never really mattered, or played a significant role in your life. When at your worst, you can be disloyal, unfaithful, untrustworthy and incredibly impractical. You lack responsibility and have a fear of commitment. People, projects and places can lack longevity too.

You invest your all in something or someone and then disregard them, a bit too easily. When imbalanced you can become highly gluttonous, either through food, any type of intoxicant, or through the excessive "consumption" of ideas, beliefs or activities. In other words, "less is more" doesn't hold any significance to you.

Impulsiveness and impatience are arguably two of your least favorable character traits. You constantly seek new experiences and connections, yet this makes you miss out on depth and authentic connections. Thus, you tend to be very superficial at times. Your 'bounce' can devolve into a lack of care or interest, and people find you frustrating and child-like. Instead of being seen as a high-spirited, liberated and colorful individual, you are seen as a child who lacks all responsibility, maturity and commitment. Your attention-span can be weak too. Distracted, careless, and lacking tact you actually annoy people when vibrating at your worst (lowest). Impatience and impulsiveness can really get the better of you. Lack of clarity and indecision can manifest through your multi-passions, so being able to pick up so many skills with ease implies that you create problems for yourself. It's part of your core nature. You struggle with focus, concentration and staying power; commitment and endurance aren't really your strength.

You struggle with staying connected to your source of personal power, instincts and internal guidance. Your intuition decreases through frivolity and moving on from people, places and projects. Anxiety can often result, but you have a hard time processing this anxiety. You don't like to accept it, in other words, and a lack of acceptance leads to rejection and suppression. A direct manifestation of this is getting involved in more projects, doing and 'busy-body' activity- which perpetuates the cycle. Your solution to being restless and experiencing the anxiety, or nervous tension, of this restlessness is to be busier and more restless! Presence suffers and you don't wish to look within to get to the core and root of problems. Another major shadow trait is not really knowing what you truly want out of life. Having so many eggs in so many baskets means that you never fully commit to anything, and never establish what your true passion or passions are in life. Again, you become a timeless and eternal wanderer. Inadequacy and insecurity can take hold if you're not careful. While you're so busy chasing the next experience your heart's desire suffers; unconsciousness takes over and conscious passions, desires, ambitions and thoughts get pushed into the unconscious, into darkness. The lowest vibration of this personality type is getting lost in drug or alcohol addiction and abuse.

In the pursuit of freedom, liberation, and a fast-paced lifestyle anger, rage and aggression can result. Cycles of emotional or physical violence can become a common occurrence, while angry bouts and frequent arguments with lovers or family can become the norm. Type 7s regularly suffer with family, friendship, money and health issues due to these tendencies. Fortunately, there are ways to overcome this as we explore in the Self-Development techniques later.

Type 7s: The Dalai Lama, Galileo Galilei, Mozart, Thoman Jefferson, Benjamin Franklin, Ram Dass, Malcolm Forbes, Chuck Berry, Miley Cyrus, Britney Spears, Russel Brand, and Sacha Baron Cohen.

Levels of Development

Healthy Levels: -

1. **When at your Best**: You live in a state of awe and wonder, inspiration and positive gratitude. You're able to assimilate new experiences with ease and teach or motivate others to connect to their own talents and passions. You're full of joy and live life in a state of emotional openness and intelligence,

abundance and spiritual illumination. You're blessed with many positive connections.

2. **Slightly below your best**: You're excitable, responsive, enthusiastic and open-minded. Gratitude flows through you and you've found your passions in life. Extroverted, spontaneous, resilient and self-empowered, you live your life with cheerfulness and zest and are open to authentic connections.

3. **Nearly there**: You're able to become an accomplished person with sufficient achievements. You're multi-talented, and although you may not have found a set path in life you are open to learning, self-development and personal growth. You have many passions and are seen as friendly, extroverted, outgoing and self-expressive.

Average levels: -

4. **On the Path**: You're restless, passionate, adventurous and free-spirited. You have many interests and intentions but don't really know what you're going to do yet, or commit to indefinitely. You like having multiple options and choices. Not too focused, slightly immature, and attracted to money, power, gadgets and "things," you are a positive and friendly individual who does well in social engagements.

5. **Learning, still in the Shadow stage**: You're hyperactive, child-like, impulsive and very spontaneous. You seek constant stimulation and distractions, you're always on the go and have very high energy levels. You're working on healing addictions and excessive tendencies and recognize a need for commitment and security in your life. Uninhibited, flamboyant, entertainer and a natural performer and wise-crack, there's a mix of positive and negative personality traits. You have many ideas, however not a great deal of follow through.

6. **Devolved**: Excess, greed, gluttony, materialism, desire and constant stimulation fills your life. You're like a kid in a candy store, a teenager who's experienced alcohol for the first time, and a child who doesn't understand 'no.' You're self-centered, demanding, unsatisfied and insensitive- with an addictive personality. Passion is starting to be steered towards talent and service, but you are not yet sure about yourself or true motivations in life.

Unhealthy levels

Impulsive, infantile, addictive and offensive… abusive, anxious, erratic and manic… supremely restless, confused, conflicted and unsure of themselves... type 7s at their lowest are the typical 'bipolar' personality. There's little to no grounding, responsibility, maturity and passions are not yet realized. Any ideas are just glimpses of 'possibilities' and 'potentials' at this stage, there isn't any true desire to take sufficient steps towards self-mastery, prosperity, success or achievement. Addictions, depression and self-destructive behaviors are common while a strong disconnection between mind, body and spirit grows.

Type 8: The Challenger

Type 8 is known as the 'Challenger.' Type 8s are bold, confident, self-assured and decisive. They possess immense inner strength and personal power, authority and force. They love to take charge and show themselves off as bosses. As an 8, you thrive in business and self-employment, also being very suited to entrepreneurship. Self-leadership and self-autonomy are two of your greatest strengths. You seek self-sufficiency and sovereignty in all aspects of life and are happy to work hard to achieve success, financial prosperity, or personal victory and accomplishment. Your charisma, charm and personal power are fine-tuned to extraordinary levels. This is the personality type that can speak in front of thousands- hundreds of thousands of people and command attention. Politicians, world leaders, nonprofit and charity leaders, international speakers and musicians are associated with the type 8 personality. When you channel your inner strength and ambition positively, you're able to achieve great success on the earthly plane. Social status, recognition and respect are important to you, you like to be seen and heart, respected and even admired.

You can be a wonderful force of change in the world. Manifestation, significant shifts, individual and collective consciousness, and world issues are all associated here. You're a visionary and idealistic with strong business acumen. Matters of wealth and money come easily to you, and you certainly aren't shy of abundance or riches. When functioning at your best, you possess an innocence that allows you to face life with an open heart, authenticity and natural desire to do good. Because you believe in success, personal accomplishment and hard-work you generally wish idealistic and inspirational ways to be widespread and available to all. This is where your innocence and power really shine through. You are a star and can work devotedly towards a cause or movement throughout a lifetime. You do not give in to cynics or unhealthy criticism too, which allows you to stay aligned to your own truth and path. You're extremely self-assured with inspiring levels of confidence and charisma. You are generous, enthusiastic, warm-hearted and independent; self-autonomous, reliable, dependable and service-oriented. Type 8's will always defend an underdog, sometimes to exemplary levels. You like to use your strength and personal power to help others- you're brave and fearless! Honorable, authoritative, respect commanding and just, you're happy to take the heat off others and face challenges to show the world the meaning of true power and strength.

Protective, supportive and community-oriented, you motivate others to realize their true potential. You're a shining light, inspirational, attractive and admirable. You can be attention-seeking, overpowering and verging on narcissistic, which we explore in your Shadow Traits, but when you're at your best you truly are a force to be reckoned with. Great success and material and financial abundance can come to a type 8 through the need to protect others and live life in an inspirational way. Combined with your intense energy and drive, ambition and highly- aspirational nature; type's 8's are and can be one of the most successful personality types. In the material and physical world, you can achieve great things and lasting change for humanity. You are generous, self-sufficient and sincere. If you can learn to balance assertion and control with cooperation and compromise, you can attune to the better aspects of your personality and self and be seen as the confident and courageous, compassionate leader that you are. Empathy is a key word for you. Developing empathy and compassion help you to maintain integrity, a very important quality with this personality type. You're decisive, strong-willed, action-oriented, and resourceful. Communication is direct, you mean what you say and say what you mean- and people sense this too. When you walk into a room or environment there is a shift in energy, you command attention and are a powerhouse.

Perceptive, intelligent, wise and discerning, this is the true personality of a leader, boss, manager or CEO. If you choose to have a family you will be a strong rock and support system for them on the practical, financial and domestic front. You know how to provide for those you love, although you will need to work on your emotional sensitivity and availability. Positively you are generous, benevolent, sincere and devoted. You possess a unique sense of creativity and innovation too. Such developed self-leadership allows you to shine in any area of life you give your time and attention to. Your inner strength is inspiring and you're tenacious, persevering, determined and magnanimous. Self-mastery is linked to the type 8 nature. You have the potential to be a pioneer, visionary leader, hero, savior, or world-class leader in your chosen field. Challenges can be faced with ease and grace, and that tenacious spirit previously mentioned. Also, many opportunities present themselves to you in life-you are a luck magnet. Resources, connections and opportunities thrive when you're being true to yourself. You believe in yourself and others, further liking to excel and master yourself, whether that be your mind, emotions, spirit, body, health, a skill set, or your finances. You're so charming with excellent communication skills that you can often persuade anyone of anything. Your willpower and vitality are deeply evolved, and you need to channel these out into the world and local communities, an 8 doesn't do so well when hiding or playing small and weak. You wish to leave your mark on the world. Endurance and tenacity are well developed.

Your primary fear and greatest desire can inspire you to be the best version of yourself. You hate being controlled; you're actually scared of it. The fear of being controlled or suppressed combined with the desire for self-control, being in charge of your own life and destiny, open doorways to opportunity and growth. Self-protection is very important to you. Self-reliance, continual self-betterment, showcasing your talents and strength, and a conscious form of 'world domination' are some of your key motivations in life. Being disrespected, offended, or harmed are no go zones and can further bring out your inner hero and boss when channeled correctly. You're an inspiring speaker, guide, teacher and way shower when acting from sincerity, altruism and kindness and integrity. Control to you applies to all aspects of your life. If you're a gardener, homemaker or small shop owner the same qualities apply, type 8 isn't just for world speakers and millionaire business wo/men! As long as you can project your power and be seen by the people you're trying to influence, the positive qualities of your personality come out. You're one of the most independent people of the Enneagram and dislike clingy, codependent and possessive people. This enables you to be a shining example of the power of self-sovereignty, healthy boundaries, and self-respect. Finally, Emotional balance and health allows you to be more resourceful, passionate, driven and ambitious, reflecting and mirroring positive strength and self-assertion. Developing emotional intelligence and sensitivity serves as magic for your already confident and head-strong personality.

Type 8 Shadow Traits

Your dark shadow traits can range from minor to quite severe. It all depends on other aspects of yourself and psyche (astrology, background, upbringing etc.). Your shadow traits are becoming the tyrant, bully and suppressor. You can be overbearing, overpowering, and unbelievably oppressive or tyrannical. You come across as arrogant, superior or confrontational quite often to occasionally, all depending on your mood and how healed or whole and balanced you are. Type 8's main shadow side is that of the bossy, controlling and overpowering bully. Instead of using your power for good you transform into a bit of a monster. Your need for control comes out and you can end up alienating even your most loyal supporters, friends or family. The shear force and will of a type 8 connected to their darkness is quite scary! Aggression, anger and impulsiveness may take over or you can simply seek to control everything and everyone around you. If you have attained a status of real influence, such as world leader, boss or CEO, manager or politician, this can be quite destructive. Logic, reason and empathy/altruism go out of the window.

In extreme cases you become vengeful, full of resentment and desires for revenge, and vindictive. You may defend yourself as much as you defend a loved one if your shadow self comes out in a dark way (unlike a type 6, who is fiercely protective of others and loved ones but less so for themselves). You don't have a problem shooting someone down (sometimes literally and not just metaphorically!) and seeking to destroy someone else. Type 8 represents the psychopath or sociopath when at their lowest. This is, of course, due to such a strong level of innate power and personal authority. You require respect, so if someone disrespects you- especially publicly- something triggers inside. Less severely, you are prone to egotistical behavior, bossiness, confrontation and extreme competitiveness. You can be incredibly infuriating to friends and family. There's no such thing as loosening control or going with the flow and being adaptable and surrendering. You're inflexible and rigid in your mindset and ways. The key thing to know is that your whole identity is tied up in your social or public image and status- self-identity is not just important to you, but it's part of your core and entire life. You're not the type of person who can quit on your life, sell your possessions and spend the rest of your life traveling the world as a nomad, for example. It's very rare for a type 8 to leave a life they've created behind.

If you can learn to balance assertion and control with cooperation and compromise, you can attune to the better aspects of your personality and self and be seen as the confident and courageous, compassionate leader that you are. Empathy, altruism, compassion and self-compassion are all essential qualities to cultivate. Your basic fear of losing control and being controlled, in addition to being harmed, can make you act in horrible and destructive ways. Immaturity, impulsive decisions, and child-like behavior can occur- temper tantrums and unforeseen outbursts alike. Or, you may resort to emotional or physical violence, blackmail or paying someone to do your dirty work. You should also look after your health. Physical burnout is common and mental, emotional, psychological and spiritual health can all suffer for a type 8. Spiritual disconnection may not be seen as important, but being overly materialistic and focused too much on practical reality can have its problems. You should seek to understand spiritual concepts and ideals more, or at least incorporate simple holistic movements and exercises into daily life. Meditation, tai chi, yoga and qigong are all ideal practices for you.

One of the worst aspects of the type 8 personality lies in your emotional disconnection. In your pursuit of power and success, personal relationships fall apart and suffer- sometimes drastically. You're so focused on making a name for yourself, becoming autonomous or prosperous, and going after your goals and aspirations that you neglect family and friends. If you've got children and a life partner there can be real internal struggles and conflicts of interest. Providing financial and practical support isn't enough, you need to be able to connect emotionally. Type 8 is quite a masculine personality... What about nurturance, care, emotional support, and showing up for your children or lover? These are important too. Your fear of being harmed extends into the fear of being hurt, yet this is just one aspect of your fear. You actually create a lot of limitations and preconceived notions and beliefs, some of which aren't true! Yes, people can be disloyal and break trust, but trust and loyalty are integral to the human experience. They're things we all have to learn at some point. You believe that your strength (of which you have a lot of) comes solely from business, monetary, financial and worldly success; yet, inner strength is built from interpersonal, intimate and loving relationships. Developing trust and emotional openness is an integral part of this. In other words, you can't close yourself off through fear of having your heart or trust broken.

Protecting yourself and your feelings is one of your main desires in life, however, what happens when you deny yourself all feelings and emotions? You become closed and cut off from both yourself and the world. And this is where the more tyrannical and oppressive aspects of your personality come into play. Working on healing yourself, strengthening family, romantic and platonic loving bonds, and making time for personal relationships will all help you greatly. Substitute keeping others at an emotional distance with emotional depth and vulnerability, release your armor. Furthermore, you must learn how to understand things instinctively and through feeling, and not just through thinking or rationalizing. Feeling VS thinking is something you have trouble with. As an 8 you believe care and support is providing gifts, resources and money, but- again- it's more about the quality time you spend with others. For such an assertive and strong character, you are incredibly sensitive and vulnerable deep down. You project your fears and insecurities outwards and find solace in your work and social status. There is an archetype of the 'workaholic' with a type 8. Make peace with feelings of shame, humiliation, and disappointment, or being judged, criticized and rejected. Try to release blocks to connection. We explore this more in the next book.

Type 8s: Franklin D Roosevelt, Winston Churchill, Oskar Schindler, Martin Luther King Jr, Indira Gandhi, Saddam Hussein, Donald Trump, Pablo Picasso, Serena Williams, Aretha Franklin, James Brown, Queen Latifah, Jack Black, Frank Sinatra, and Clint Eastwood.

Levels of Development

Healthy Levels: -

1. **When at your Best**: You're magnanimous, courageous, inspirational and an amazing role model or leader. People look up to you for your confidence, self-assurity and inner strength. You radiate personal power and work towards creating a better world- you have vision and genuine passion to serve. This is the vibration of historical greatness, of creating a legacy and lasting change.

2. **Slightly below your best**: You're recognized for your talents and service to others or society. You've already accomplished a considerable amount and live with passion, integrity and presence. You're decisive, strong-willed, driven and honorable. A natural leader, people look up to you and you're considered a champion of the people.

3. **Nearly there**: You're self-assertive, driven, ambitious and confident. You ooze bravery and courage and have your eye on the prize. You're committed to reaching the top and are making sacrifices to get there. Passionate, resourceful and authoritative, you can be ruthless and relentless in your aspirations and

actions but are equally seen and loved. Your heart shines through.

Average levels: -

4. **On the Path**: You're self-sufficient, financially independent, hard-working and risk taking. You know where you're going and what you need to do to get there. Personal relationships can suffer, and you're not entirely emotionally balanced, but you're pragmatic, positive and self-empowered.

5. **Learning, still in the Shadow stage**: You're dominating and controlling while being inspiring simultaneously. You alternate between your best (light) and worst (shadow) qualities. You're very ambitious, focused on control and success, and forceful. Positively you're supportive, encouraging, and motivating. Negatively you're proud, egotistical, boastful and imposing. You've yet to transcend the shadow attributes of your personality, yet possess vision and foresight.

6. **Devolved**: Confrontational, intimidating, power-hungry and controlling, people haven't seen your true potential yet. You come across as angry and belittling instead of wise and inspiring. You can be threatening and tyrannical to get your way, or a bit of a

diva (without the accomplishment, fame or success to back it up!). You sort of know yourself but have a long way to go; you're aware of your light and greatness however don't know how to express it properly, yet.

Unhealthy levels

Ruthless, dictatorial, tyrannical, immoral and unjust, you're a bully and quite soulless. Your personal power and internal force is being expressed in all the wrong ways. Violence, aggression and manipulation are common. A type 8 at this stage is the typical con artist, outlaw, criminal and renegade. You believe you're invincible and are generally reckless, self-destructive, destructive, sociopathic and anti-social.

Type 9: The Peacemaker

Type 9's are known as Peacemakers and Mediators. They are lovers of harmony, cooperation and compromise, balance, unity and compassionate relating. This is the most spiritual personality type of all the 9 Enneatypes. Unconditional love, compassion and empathy come very natural to them; they are characterized by an easy-going, down-to-earth and understanding nature. If you are a type 9, you are deeply concerned with justice and morality, and with cooperation and unity (or lack of).

Relationships are important to you and you are sweet, nurturing, caring and attentive. Social justice, fairness and human rights, and all aspects of harmony and balance concern a type 9. You're suited to a counselling, caring, mediation or diplomacy role and professional path. Psychic, spiritual, intuitive, imaginative and empathic gifts are strong too. This type is very similar to type 6 and a lot of what was said there applies here. Specifically, for type 9, you avoid conflict and work towards peace as best as possible. This strong aversion to conflict and arguments can inspire you to achieve extraordinary levels of compassion, empathy, compromise and selflessness. When channeled positively you are a force to be reckoned with- not through physical stamina and strength, but through a subtle yet deeply moving inner strength. Spirit flows through you powerfully. You're humanitarian, altruistic, generous and gifted in the realms of the imagination, clairvoyant, and artistic.

You do need to be careful of avoidance and escapism, however when at your best you're able to accomplish great things and make some wonderful connections. People see you as a sparkling, sincere and spiritually insightful being. You're wise, intuitive, and possessing soul-depth and intimacy are apparent within you. The type 9 personality is balanced at the top and center of the Enneagram, meaning you have both a highly grounding quality and are often people's gem or rock. You are receptive, agreeable, compromising and understanding, and also highly compassionate and empathetic. In fact, you are literally the peacemaker signifying that you are defined by idealism, a sense of unconditional love, and a desire to do the right thing. But you're not "away with the fairies," you're grounded and in tune with both your body and the world. Physical environments are important to you, so even if you feel an affinity with emotions and bonding through shared spiritual or emotional values, you still like to keep things rooted in material reality. Sincere and amazingly selfless you can often sacrifice your own wants, needs and personal desires to create unity and harmony for everyone. You're a natural diplomat and mediator and often find strangers gravitating towards you for your unique listening skills, and for your wisdom.

Self-acceptance and self-awareness are two of your greatest qualities. You're balanced, perceptive, instinctual and evolved spiritually. You're actually an *advanced soul*. 9 represents completion, you can be seen as the personality most embodying spiritual completion. You're able to rise above the individual "I" and egocentric reality to attain new heights within and around. You're selfless, inspiring, charismatic and devoted. Bold and brave too, you possess a magnetic quality that radiates out to affect people and places surrounding you. Your aura is strong! Transcendence is a keyword with type 9. Many type 9s can transcend the limits of this 3-dimensional reality to access the divine. This signifies that music, meditation and healing can be a mystic or transcendental experience for you- which further enhances your empathy and selfless wisdom. You're receptive, agreeable, reassuring and generous in your time, energy, wisdom and affections; you truly are a gem to others. In addition to being a diplomat and mediator, you're also a dreamer at heart. You have the ability of tuning into the subconscious realms for deep insight and self-discovery. Dreams serve as inspiration and a glimpse into your soul, psyche, and hidden unseen desires.

Your energy is down-to-earth and modest. But you're not just spiritual, ethereal and subconsciously connected- you're also creatively gifted and "supercharged." What does this mean? It signifies that you have lots of energy, passion and vitality. You're full of optimism and creative inspiration. Because you're a very grounded person you are reliable and dependable. You are trustworthy, practical, and materially and spiritually balanced. This is a beautiful way to be... It allows you to connect to both the subtle realms of spirit, the universe and source, astral and ethereal energy where insight and ideas into consciousness are rich; and to physical and material structures and foundations. You use and appreciate the physical tools and resources available to you, therefore you may find yourself achieving considerable success and accomplishment in the world if you should choose to. At your best you are all-embracing, self-sacrificing (to a healthy extent) and healing.

Speaking of healing, you also have a healing presence. Many natural and spiritual healers are associated with type 9. Alternatively, you project an aura of warmth, emotional openness, and non-judgement. Many people feel you are an alien of sorts! This is a positive thing. Your frequency is attuned to one of empathy and universal, unconditional compassion. It's beautiful and rare. You're able to bring people to give and heal others through your kindness, wisdom, presence or deep intuitive insights. It's often like you have a direct cord or link to the universe, in fact. You speak with such depth and wisdom that you might become a guide, astrologer, tarot reader, or medium. Channeling divine wisdom and benevolent forces come naturally to you. You're a spiritual seeker, a child of the universe, and fascinated by the cosmos, celestial activity, and the stars. Past life memories or "unexplainable" phenomena may come rather effortlessly. You are more intuitive and right-brain than you are left, with the right brain being related to 'free flow' of information and ideas, the imagination, creativity, instincts and intuition. Instinctively you feel into people, places and situations, a gift so advanced it can be considered telepathy (telepathic communication). Like dolphins that speak through supersonic sound waves, bats who use echolocation to see in the dark, and snakes sensing subtle vibrations, type 9s are gifted with an evolved form of empathy; the ability to know exactly what it's like to be in another's shoes. This allows you to see, hear, smell, sense and taste on a whole new level. You understand on an instinctive level, i.e. you share feelings and thoughts.

On a physical level, you heal conflicts and can help even the most opposing parties find common ground, or see sense. You seek peace in all you do and motivate others to take a leaf out of your book. You possess tremendous power and personal magnetism. Your strength is instinctual yet intuitive, physical but mental, and grounded and spiritually in tune. You can carry many feelings, impressions, beliefs, emotions, perspectives and stories along with you rather effortlessly. If an analogy were to be used to describe you, you would be seen as a pristinely clean and pure river, with extensions out into the ocean and sea and smallest lakes and streams equally. You're interconnected, connected to the world around you and the waters within simultaneously. Graceful, pure, honest, sincere and a believer in hope and faith, you carry the unique vibration of spiritual illumination. You're deep and authentic and are far from superficial, shallow and frivolous. Due to being at the top of Enneagram you can be seen as the *Crown*. The crown, of course, symbolizes nobility, spiritual enlightenment, universal truth and a majestic vibe. You're also a bit of a chameleon!

How does this manifest? Firstly, you can be a social butterfly. But it also means you embody some of the positive strengths and traits of all the other 8 Enneatypes. You're blessed with the strength of 8, the sense of adventure and fun of 7, the service and selflessness of 6, the intellectualism of 5, the creativity of 4, the freedom and glow of 3, the empathy and generosity of 2, and the idealism and pioneerism of 1. To conclude... Your basic fear is loss and separation. Your primary desire in life is to find inner stability and security, and peace of mind. You want to create harmonious environments and bring people together in unity and divine union. Seeking to avoid conflict and tension can lead you to become the most powerful, compassionate and inspiring version of yourself. Charisma, empathy, clarity and self-esteem flow through you.

Type 9 Shadow Traits

In order to keep the peace, you can often sacrifice yourself. This includes your wants, desires and personal needs or aspirations. Having such a strong aversion to conflict, arguments and tension ultimately means you tend to sacrifice yourself, and this is seldom healthy. As a result, you simplify problems, resort to escapism or denial, or become complacent. You find an illusory sense of comfort or solace in the things that are right and wonderful in your world, yet you overlook the bad. There are issues in life, type 9. Some things can't be pushed under the carpet or dismissed so easily. Tension is a chance for growth and learning, self-development and personal transformation, so how can you expect to grow and evolve if you don't want to face problems head on? Complacency isn't the best option for you. A false sense of security can manifest. Fortunately, you hold and embody a very high vibration and one of spiritual illumination and maturity. You therefore tend to be extremely protected throughout life. In saying this, it would still benefit you to challenge yourself and not always play the peacemaker, or sacrifice for the benefit of all parties involved. Try and swap complacency for action and self-assertion.

You want everything to go smoothly, which is a beautiful trait, and you genuinely wish for peace, harmony and universal love and compassion for all. But issues in health and wellbeing and your personal life can take hold if you're not careful. Self-sacrifice is arguably one of your worst traits, and your aversion to conflict. The other is inertia, stubbornness and laziness- idleness and apathy. You can become lost in stagnation, in a lack of movement and forward progression. Momentum is lost, passion decreases, and problems in self-esteem and self-worth start to take over. This occurs when you've succumbed to too much repression, denial or simplification of issues. You become lazy, lethargic and idle, relationships, projects and passion pursuits stop, and you can get into a rut quite quickly. Mild or more severe forms of depression can form. There is an inability to face responsibility- putting your game face on can be quite difficult if you've been stuck in a rut for some time. Avoidance and aversion to conflict also result in diminished duty and responsibility.

Ambivalence, over-sensitivity, emotionalism and apathy are other key issues. You may frequently resort to fantasies and emotional constructs; getting lost or preoccupied in dream worlds are common, as is actual fantasy and excessive daydreaming. It's okay for your mind to wander and to be imaginative, but being unable to distinguish reality from illusion is a problem. So long as you still know the difference you are alright! Also, because you are so instinctive and instinctual, when you're out of balance you can unconsciously put yourself in a rut. You block your own power- either because it's too much to handle, too intense, etc.- and make sure your psyche is temporarily idle and inert. Again, this isn't the best way to handle such intense personal power and psychic-spiritual gifts. You would be better off engaging in rest and relaxation, allowing yourself time to completely unwind and express yourself however you wish (whether that be through art, music, movies, gardening, meditation, sleep, cooking, creativity, etc.). The other option is to be more physical, exercise and move more- type 9 is an instinctive and spiritual personality type, so you sometimes struggle with physical movement. Physical movement helps ideas, impressions and emotions to move too.

Despite embodying qualities from all 9 personality types you have a problem with self-identity. This largely comes from your spiritual and psychological gifts. You don't possess a strong sense of self-identity; it's not that you don't *"know thyself"* - because you do, it's just that you're so peace-seeking you try and be everything and nothing simultaneously. This isn't the nihilism as seen earlier in another personality type, this is more on the wavelength of 'numbing out,' connecting to nothingness in an interconnected and "I am connected to everything, life, the universe itself; Spirit" sort of way. You become one with everything and Creation itself. This isn't inherently bad, but it can be negative if you don't do it in a way that supports personal growth or self-realization. There's a sense of emptiness and nothingness you can reach which leads to either epic self-realization, divine alignment, and spiritual awareness- or inertia, stagnation and depression. Why might you steer towards the latter? You feel pain and suffering on a deep level. Your advanced compassion and empathy makes you open to suffering, trauma and pain many humans can't comprehend. Again, denial and repression or pain/conflict avoidance might take over.

Be mindful of genuine transcendence & spiritual unification and escapism. We all have an inner darkness, life itself involves darkness; but, your key is to not get lost in the darkness or emptiness. Try not to escape into premature Buddhahood or white light (the divine, spiritual realms) as a sole coping mechanism. Adopting the mantra *'the only way is through'* would benefit you greatly. Loss and separation can inspire you when channeled and expressed helpfully, and your main motive in life- to attain inner stability and peace of mind- enables you to be mindful of your shadow tendencies in order to integrate their wisdom and embody more light. We're not saying it's easy for you, but being so spiritually inclined allows you to embrace the darkness, emptiness and suffering of life in a way others can't, and thus *alchemize* it into something beautiful, inspiring and self-empowering.

Type 9s: Queen Elizabeth II, Princess Grace of Monaco, Claude Monet, Abraham Lincoln, Dwight Eisenhower, Carl Jung, Walt Disney, Carlos Santana, Jack Johnson, and Whoopie Goldberg.

Levels of Development

Healthy Levels: -

1. **When at your Best**: You're self-autonomous, positive and optimistic, self-sovereign and gifted in many areas. Compassionate, empathic, intuitive and deeply connected to your instincts, you are a force of nature and of the universe. You possess equanimity and contentment and are at one with yourself. Relationships are supportive and blissful, and you feel intensely alive, connected and self-expressive. Life is a beautiful dream!

2. **Slightly below your best**: You're deeply receptive, emotionally intelligent, good-natured and generous. Unpretentious,

trusting, accepting and spiritual, you treat others how you wish to be treated. You're a beautiful person capable of selflessness, empathy and innocence.

3. **Nearly there**: You're optimistic, at ease with yourself, warm-hearted and genuine in your actions and intentions. You have some minor issues you need to work on, but relationships generally tend to serve as a reflection to your heart and higher self. You're supportive and have a healing nature which others appreciate.

Average levels: -

4. **On the Path**: You're free of conflicts and materialist desire, but accommodating and appeasing. You're philosophical and wise however tend to idealize people and situations. You tend to fall into the conventional roles and expectations of others. Nethertheless, you're on your way to becoming an excellent communicator and mediator.

5. **Learning, still in the Shadow stage**: You're complacent, unresponsive, unreflective and disengaged from others and yourself. You sweep problems under the rug and are lazy, anti-self-development, and prone to fantasy.

You tune out problems and are only slightly connected to your beautiful gifts and inner light.

6. **Devolved**: You're appeasing, people-pleasing and very indifferent to problems and real-world matters, including practicalities. Wishful thinking and not being able to take conscious action are common- you believe in 'magical solutions' appearing without taking any steps. Anger, frustration, and procrastination are common.

Unhealthy levels

Repressed, devolved, spiritually disconnected and escapist, unhealthy 9s avoid all of their problems. They're ungrounded and neglectful, lacking all practical duties and responsibility- to self and others. Blocking emotions, feelings and sensations are a common experience and you become numb, depersonalized and disoriented. Self-abandonment, retreating into a shell, extreme codependency and multiple personalities are associated here. It's hard to function in the real world and eating disorders, repressed anger, addictions and anxiety develop.

Chapter 3: Enneagram Self-Discovery

Spiritual Illumination and Self-Realization

The Enneagram has been created and adapted from spiritual and religious traditions. Self-realization and spiritual illumination are integral to the Enneagram system of self-discovery. Now you're familiar with the 9 main personality types, it's useful to be aware of the other significant aspects. These are Virtues, Passions, Holy Ideas and Ego-Fixations. These are based on the idea of their being a "divine form" and "holy essence" to life, and to our core natures.

The *Holy Ideas* are the higher aspects of yourself relating to the higher mind, or *Higher Self.* The Higher Self is in opposition to the Lower Self, the part of self and personality responsible for our inner animal instincts and passions, and our untamed, raw and primal feelings and emotions. The Higher Self relates to our intuition and connection to the divine. Each Holy Idea has a corresponding *Virtue*, which are qualities of the heart symbolized by pure and positive emotions, such as love, empathy, kindness, and generosity. When we lose self- awareness and presence the positive attributes of the Holy Idea transform into our egotistical characteristics. These are also known as the **Ego-Fixations**. Simultaneously, losing touch with your Virtue can create the associated characteristics of **Passion**. Passions are our untamed, primal and animal nature often described as the "Lower Self," as previously mentioned, or at least aspects of it. Instinct replaces intuition- a quality associated with the higher self and symbolizing our gut feelings and *inner knowing-* and all aspects of higher connection and awareness, divinity, and spiritual contact are replaced.

It is our innate and fundamental connection to 'soul' that allows us to connect to the Holy Ideas and Virtues, whereas it is our natural tendencies and drive towards our "inner animals," our instinctual, primal and human selves that equally create the Ego-Fixations and Passions. Being aware of these can help you on your journey to spiritual enlightenment, self-development, and personal growth and transformation. Knowing your personality type allows you to increase presence and higher awareness, so you can learn to contemplate and embody the higher qualities of your true self, further developing empathy.

Let's look at the specifics in relation to each personality type. The order expressed is:
Holy Idea, Virtue... Passion, Ego-Fixation.

1. Type 1: Perfection, Serenity... Anger, Resentment
2. Type 2: Will/Freedom, Humility... Pride, Flattery
3. Type 3: Hope, Truthfulness... Deceit, Vanity
4. Type 4: Origin, Equanimity/Calm... Envy, Melancholy
5. Type 5: Transparency, Non-attachment/Selflessness... Greed, Stinginess
6. Type 6: Faith, Courage... Fear, Cowardice
7. Type 7: Wisdom/Plan, Sobriety... Gluttony, Planning
8. Type 8: Truth, Innocence... Lust, Vengeance
9. Type 9: Love, Action... Slothfulness, Indolence/Laziness

The Holy Ideas

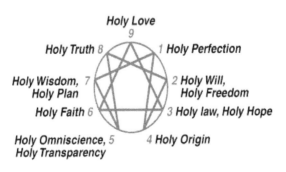

Oscar Ichazo's Enneagram of the Holy Ideas.
Copyrighted Image: "Enneagram Institute."

Each Holy Idea also has a corresponding Virtue. The loss of awareness of the Holy Idea becomes a person's Ego-fixation. While we all have the capacity to embody all of the Holy Ideas, only one of them is central to the soul's destiny. The loss of one's Holy Idea is felt most acutely and profoundly, and further leads to one's ego becoming preoccupied with trying to recreate it. If we lose our center- our Holy Idea- and become distorted in our thinking, feeling, and actions and behaviors, the "lower," "lesser," and shadow/unhealthy aspects of personality and self, start to take center-stage. Thus, we begin to forget our connection to the divine.

"An essential individual will be in contact with these (Virtues) constantly, simply by living in his body. But the subjective individual, the ego, loses touch with these Virtues. Then the personality tries to compensate by developing passions." (*Interviews with Oscar Ichazo, page 19*).

The Virtues

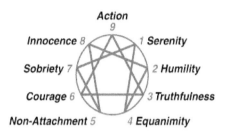

Oscar Ichazo's Enneagram of the Virtues. *Copyrighted Image: "Enneagram Institute."*

Each Holy Idea also has a corresponding Virtue, or, in other words, each Virtue will be linked to a main archetype of self-known as the Holy Idea. The Virtues are essential qualities of the heart experienced by all human beings when we are abiding in "essence," our true selves. The loss of contact and connection with the Virtue causes the person's corresponding Passion. This happens when a person loses awareness and presence, falling away from their true core and becoming disconnected from one's essence. While everyone has the capacity to embody all of the Virtues, like with the Holy Idea, only one of them is central to the soul's identity.

The loss of one's Virtue is felt most acutely, and the person's ego is most preoccupied with recreating it, although in a self-defeating and inharmonious to 'self' way. Again, the Passion is often the result. The Virtues describe the expansive, non-dual qualities of "essence" experienced in a direct way, and are further the *natural* expressions of the awakened heart. Virtues are not forced, i.e. we do not force ourselves to be "virtuous." Instead, as we relax and become more present and awake, seeing through the fears and desires of the ego self, the qualities of our Virtue naturally manifest.

The Passions

Oscar Ichazo's Enneagram of the Passions. *Copyrighted Image: "Enneagram Institute."*

Your Passion arises once you have begun to truly lose touch with your essence, your true self and Virtue. The Passion is the primal, "inner animal" aspect of self. To many psychoanalysts and key thinkers in modern times this is equated with the "shadow self," or the key shadow personality traits. The Passions are the undesirable, seemingly dark or denied aspects of personality and self. They are seen as in opposition to the divine and represent the lower human characteristic. While everyone has the capacity to embody all of the Passions only one of them is central to the soul's and your spirit's identity. The Passions represent an underlying *emotional response* to reality created by the loss of contact with our Essential nature, with the core and grounding of our Being, with our true identity as Spirit or essence. The underlying hurt, pain, loss and grief or shame that this loss brings are large and significant, and our ego is compelled to come up with a particular way of emotionally coping with the loss. This temporarily effective, but ultimately misguided coping strategy which can also lead to many self-destructive behaviors and tendencies, is the Passion. Because the Passion is a distortion of an innate essential Virtue, recognizing the Passion can help us to restore the Virtue.

The Ego-Fixations

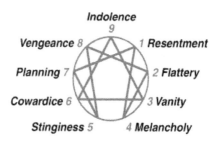

Oscar Ichazo's Enneagram of the Ego-Fixations.
Copyrighted Image: "Enneagram Institute."

As the Holy Ideas represent specific non-dual aspects of the core personality (essence), the *loss* of the Holy Idea leads to the Ego-Fixation. The Holy Ideas arise and are embodied when one's mind is clear, calm and in tune with the higher self or mind (or the divine), therefore the loss of/ disconnection from this creates an "ego- delusion" known as this Ego-Fixation. Through the Ego-Fixation, one is trying to restore the balance and freedom of the Holy Idea, but due to the dualistic perspective of the ego, cannot. Again, understanding the perspective of our type's Holy Idea functions as an antidote to the Ego-Fixation, so recognizing the Ego-Fixation can help us to restore the Holy Idea. As there is a specific relationship between the higher qualities of the self and soul and the corresponding "ego distortions," developing presence and awareness through meditation, mindfulness and empathy can help you overcome the Ego-Fixation and rise to meet your own Holy Idea (and Virtue) within. Your Essence is limited by the Ego-Fixation, just as your Virtue is limited by your Passion.

Finally (and this is true with all of the subcategories of self) knowing one's "type" is a direct and powerful way to influence inner work to facilitate the transformative process. Healing, spiritual development, and the embodiment of empathy and other qualities in alignment with "essence," can all be expanded through learning about your Personality type.

Chapter 4: Healing and Self-Development with the Enneagram

Self-Development Tips, Techniques & Advice

You will already be familiar with the 9 Enneatypes, including both their light and positive qualities and dark and shadow traits. Now we are going to go into self-development tips, techniques and wisdom for healing and integration. Remember that the Enneagram is all about *self-realization*, it's about integrating the light aspects of your personality while seeking to let go of the negative shadow personality traits. It is not about repression or denial, however. In order to find the light you must first make peace with your inner darkness. The shadow self serves as guidance into how you can best find the light; what you need to do to transcend the limitations or restrictions of your personality, and further how you can begin your own journey of healing, recovery and returning to wholeness.

Type 1

Re-cap of key Shadow Traits to overcome:-

- Judgement, intolerance and uncompromisable.
- Dogmatic and pushy, believing you're always right.
- Self-criticism and extreme need for perfectionism.
- Overly-analytical, feel the need to explain and defend yourself, and control everything and everyone around you.

It's important that you take time to relax and engage in pure, liberated rejuvenation. You are prone to burn out, so 'taking a chill pill' metaphorically speaking, and adopting an easy-going attitude, are essential for you. As the reformer and activist who strives towards idealism, making the world and society a better place, *balancing work, rest and play* is honestly the best thing you could do for yourself. It sounds so simple yet just this one change will produce catalytic shifts, shifts in your well-being, mindset, health and ability to experience joy and pleasure on a daily basis. Relationships will get a boost too, you'll also find yourself better able to communicate and stand strong in your morals and personal convictions. Cultivating patience will help you to overcome the need to become dogmatic, self-righteous and obsessive in your pursuits for pushing your purpose on others. As an instinctive and Gut centre enneatype, you have a very direct approach. But your instincts don't always serve you well because you don't know how to relax. You're therefore attuned to a vibration (frequency) of 'do, do, do!' Patience can be cultivated by spending more time connecting to your hearts, emotions and inner empathy. Having compassion for others will instantly initiate a process of patience and tolerance. Compassion is the seed of nurturance, kindness and of course patience. Spend time by bodies of water such as lakes, oceans, rivers and even ponds. Reflect and introspect- *slow down*... Journaling every day would be a great way to make sense of such intense emotions and motivations, and why you project them in the way you do.

Remember that it can be difficult for you to follow your instincts and feelings. I know, this sounds like a contradiction; you're the most instinctive person, right? Well, you tend to be in your mind, attuned to the mental and psychological planes and modes of being. This makes you fall short in emotions, feelings, *conscious* instinctual responses, and physical and spiritual necessities. Sports and exercise will help you to feel more connected to your body, and subsequent instincts. You're naturally instinctive and intuitive, it's just that you overthink and rationalize yourself out of your gut feelings and ability to connect with others. You should be more active on purely a physical level, i.e. not just be active if it's to pursue your goals or idealistic pursuits. If traditional sports and gym don't interest you, take regular long walks in nature, dance to your favorite tunes, engage in yoga or tai chi, and take up martial arts. Even activities like frisbee or swimming for fun and pleasure are significant! You need to learn how to change your systematic and purposeful approach to everything- exercise and movement included- into an act of pleasure. For example, instead of getting up to go for a run or jog, or yoga, solely to feed your work and ability to perform in your profession, do these things to serve yourself. Joy, pleasure, and activities that you can call 'fun' are ideal for you.

Change the way you see things. A shift in mindset is sometimes all it takes and this is especially true for you. Instincts drive your life, you're certainly not lacking in inspiration or purpose, so try to merge these powerful inner forces with the positive path of pleasure. Looking at the symbolism and energetic meanings of Venus will really benefit you. Venus is the planet of beauty, sensuality, fmeinine energy and sexality, luxury and wealth. Also pleasure. Venus inspires us to connect to our inner divine feminine energy, regardless of being a man or woman. This includes the qualities of romance, nurturance, empathy, gentleness, receptivity and passivity. Connecting to your inner Venus enables you to slow down, be more soft and gentle in approach, and self-indulge. Beauty, luxury and sensuality won't take away from your goals- if anything, they'll actually inspire you more; they'll just do so in a way that adds to your personal magnetism. This then allows you to relate to others better, in a more empathic, authentic and cooperative way. Venus is a planet of cooperation, love and harmony. It's also interesting to note that Venus is the opposite to Mars, the planet of war, aggression, lust and action. Mars represents primal instincts, competition, vitality and immense passion, but this can often come out in angry, impulsive and extremely competitive ways (for anyone with a lot of Mars energy & influence).

To connect to your spiritual side, make a conscious effort to incorporate meditation and spiritual healing or therapy into your lifestyle. Just 10 minutes of meditation in the morning and evening, or before bed, will work wonders. Unconscious impulses can be activated through movement and spiritual healing. We are more than our bodies, we are spiritual creatures having a human experience! Alternatively, if you're someone who considers yourself quite spiritual and ethereal (you dream a lot, are connected to the astral and subtle realms, etc.) remember that you may be a soul, but you also have a body. Blocks to instinctual awareness can arise from a number of different paths. Being so over-analytical and judgemental can lead to bouts of aggression. You tend to be competitive and dogmatic or pushy, and this can lead to sexual aggression at times. Emotions thus suffer. To find emotional balance and serenity in addition to bonding with people on a harmonious sexual level, do the following. Tantra is a great way to reconnect with your mind, body & spirit. Tantric philosophy advocates that sex and intimacy should be a holistic act; we shoul engage with our lover or lovers on a mental/psycholgcial, emotional, phsycial and spiritual level. Sex is an act of love which can raise your vibration and connect you to your heart space, where love, peace, tolerance, empathy and compassion reign. Tantric sexuality or breathwork increases your capacity for deep and heart-centred connections. They both (breathwork and then sharing intimacy with a partner) result in more intimate and authentic bonds while opening doorways to vulnerability. You may think you are emotionally available and even vulnerable at times because you care so much and feel so deeply, but you don't show this in the way you may believe you do. Meditation, breathwork and tantric philosophy will assist you in overcoming this distortion and internal block.

Finally, as someone who is naturally instinctive (when at your best) you need to be careful of not letting your instincts and emotions control you. The other side of being disconnected from your instincts is being too reliant on them. This can lead to lust, primal fears manifesting as aggression and becoming overpowering, and getting out of touch and tune with your positive reformistic and idealistic qualities. Consider journaling and writing down your thoughts and feelings. Self-expression is an amazing way to release past wounds and pain- trauma responses often stay with us for years & years to come... Anger builds up when you don't come to terms with sensations of injustice and wrongdoing, so you may 'explode' from time to time. "Self righteous anger" is justifiable, however how are you expressing it?! In a healthy way? In a way that supports your growth and empowers you? Your needs and feelings are important. Go in and through to come out and up. Resistance is futile, it leads to more of what you don't want. Nature therapy is almost essential for you.

Type 2

Re-cap of key Shadow Traits to overcome:-

- People-pleasing, appeasing and self-sacrificing.
- Repress your own needs to help or support others; subservient.
- Codependency- clingy and unhealthy behaviors.
- Over time, built up frustrations and resentment which can lead to anger and imbalances.
- Pride, arrogance and low self-esteem as a sort of "trigger response."

Your main goal in life is to work out how to balance your own needs with caring for others. You're a nurturer and caregiver, you seek to help loved ones and strangers in any way possible. But this leaves you depleted, self-sacrificing and drained which in turn lead to a number of other problems. Make a mantra along the lines of, *"I cannot help or serve others if I don't serve myself.... My needs are important- I honor my personal dreams, ambitions, emotions and desires."* Mantras and affirmations are a great way to engage in self-development. They allow you to make your intentions known and actively reshape and restructure physical matter.

146

Mind affects matter. Mantras are a sort of self-affirmation whereby you declare your intentions to the universe (and to yourself). They help to raise your vibration and overall frequency, which, on a subtle level, break down energy blockages, faulty beliefs systems and distorted mindsets. Thought and emotional patterns are positively impacted by mantras. In a way, it is a type of neurolinguistic programming! Self-care and rest are extremely important for you too. Without them, you are an emotional wreck, also prone to breakdowns and stress, self-delusions and trigger responses; reaction instead of responding. Spending time in nature or immersing yourself in music or art therapy are ideal ways to restore personal energy levels. Type 2's are a bit like empaths. You give, help and nurture to the point of neglecting your own needs. So, change the way you see yourself and your role here. Being your own best friend, healer and therapist will outshine the need to be everyone else's. Even taking one or two small steps are steps inthe right direction; commit to change and help *yourself.*

Become conscious of your motives. Writing down your intentions through journaling or mindful introspection and contemplation helps you to release unresolved and tricky emotions. A lot of what we hold onto is unconscious, or subconscious, i.e. it is below the level of consciousness (our conscious

147

minds). This means we react and not respond or become angry, frustrated, sad, wounded or triggered without realizing why. Being so giving in nature means you close yourself off to receiving. Further, the yin and yang symbol is something you should include at home or in your office, or potentially draw. Sit down and draw the yin and yang symbol as a type of therapy. Yin is receptive, feminine and passive in nature while yang is active, masculine and dominant. Together, they bring wholeness and unity, they form consciousness and creation. Yin and yang are ultimately the opposing, yet complementary forces of creation and the universe, residing within all things. This universal symbol will help you to open up to receiving, whether that be love, gifts, blessings, affection, wisdom and advice- anything you need. Whatever you give in generosity and abundance you should equally receive. Meditating on yin and yang enables you to recognize where you have been out of balance, where you've been giving too much of yourself away, and how you can overcome it. The yin and yang symbol serves as a gateway or energetic portal to higher levels of self-realization and healing. Health and well-being can be restored this way.

Also, are you 'giving' to 'expect' something in return? The other side of your personality is becoming manipulative or fake- you start to give with expectation. Unconscious codependent patterns can emerge as a result. Appreciation diminishes too, and this can lead to poverty consciousness, being in a state of lack, want and need. Count your blessings. Practice gratitude daily, a shrine or altar would help you significantly. Place things on your shrine or altar that remind you of the beauty of the universe. You might want to consider putting things from all the elements, like a candle for fire, shell or bowl of water for water, crystal or gemstone for earth, and feather for air. Then, supercharge your altar with religious or spiritual symbols, pictures and deities that remind you of gratitude and abundance, divinity and grace. Even 5- 10 minutes (daily) sitting in meditative contemplation at your altar will help you significantly. You feel things very deeply as a type 2, and no-one can question your advanced levels of kindness, caring and genuine desire to nurture and provide. However, being so "extreme" leads to its polarity. Are you familiar with the concept of duality? Because you're a Heart centre enneatype you reach out to the world through feelings and emotions, subtle impressions and your heart. But this neglects the other aspects of self, the Gut (instincts) and Head (mind- thoughts & logic). You're unable to observe the world and think rationally or directly engage with the others in a practical and direct way.

Submissiveness and this extremist need to nurture and emotionalize can be eased through working on your instincts, intuition and mind. Cerebral qualities lead to intellectual connection, and intellectual and mental connection naturally reduce such a strong emphasis on emotions. Coming to terms with duality as a metaphysical concept, and your own polarities and dual nature within is an ideal self-development route. Visualization meditation will help you overcome codependency and any potential disappointment you feel when people say no to your help. Learn how to ask questions: 'Do you need help?' 'Would you like me to do this?' 'Can I…?' This sets you up for both success and self-realization, and personal growth and independence. Either way, you win or learn something. Self-love and self-care should be on your agenda.. Give yourself daily massages; burn essential oils in oil diffusers; play sweet and soulful, healing and uplifting tunes and music that soothes you, and immerse yourself in artistic and creative expression. Self-expression that lets your inner child and imagination run free reminds you of your source of personal power. It assists in self-alignment and healing, overcoming wounds, insecurities and intense emotions or sensitivities.

The power of connecting with your inner child shouldn't go undervalued. Due to being so nurturing and caring, you often take on the role of provider, care-giver, or mother. Mothers are beautiful and amazing goddesses, but they can also be dominating, authoritative and coercive- not to mention then feeling used, taken for granted and all the rest of it. Resentment is a reality. There is such a thing as family and ancestral karma as well; the wounds and trauma-response and 'triggers' that build up when having so much pressure and responsibility to care for others. Like empaths, you lose boundaries and let in things that don't belong to you, or at the very least feel weighed down and as if you have way too many duties. Commiting to a bi-annual retreat, spa weekend, spiritual pilgrimage or break are *perfect* choices. On a more frequent basis, dedicate to doing something just for you, for your needs and well-being. This can be anything from a quiet night in to pampering yourself, enjoying your own company, and watching a movie or chilling out with a book.

Type 3

Re-cap of key Shadow Traits to overcome:-

- Constant need for approval, admiration and recognition, or to impress others.
- Fake, superficial and materialistic.
- Alienate people and disconnect from emotional needs (in your desire for success, fame or power).

- Overthinking, lack of feeling, and lack of presence; always living in the future.
- Overly competitive, arrogant, narcissistic, impatient and lacking grace and tact.

Your main challenge is to learn how to be at peace with yourself, gifts and talents, without needing recognition or praise. This is one of the most narcissistic personality types when left unchecked. What's the opposite of narcissism? Empathy, humility and grace... Meditation and spiritual healing are two of the fastest roots back to yourself. You are naturally creative, multi-talented and artistically gifted; you're innovative and high-flying. So why not tune into these in a positive way? Express yourself. Find ways to energize your gifts and soul talents on a daily basis. Combine it with meditation and *mindfulness*, acts of being conscious and present- i.e. not thinking into the future or looking back at the pat, and you will see significant change. Mindfulness is being present with yourself. When you're present you are living in the moment, you're not too far in the past or future where you lose touch with yourself. Most to all issues in communication and relationship breakdowns occur because one is not being present with their feelings, emotions and immediate environment. Learn how to only look back at past failures or accomplishments to help or benefit you now. Don't dwell on shortcomings, as you'll get stuck there. And try not to be too attached to wins and victories *unless* it can lead to self-development and healthy joy in the present. Presence is key for you. Because your enneatype is a Heart type, you reach out to the world based on a vibration that is in harmony with your inner life and being. Inner impressions, inner feelings, inner beliefs... these are reflected outwards.

So, be mindful of the other aspects of yourself: your mind and instincts. Instead of just being concerned with *reaching out* to the world, try to *directly engage* and *interact*. This is something 'Gut' types don't have a problem with. Work on self-assertion and masculine traits and qualities. Simultaneously, seek to incorporate the qualities of your mind and the 'Head' centre. Logic, reason and observation can help you go a long way. Thinking rationally and intuitively allows you to ground your charm and pragmatism in an empowering and productive, but equally interconnected, way. Think in terms of connection with a recognition of holism. We are beings of mind, body & spirit; you may relate with others and the world emotionally, yet many other people resonate with intellectual and cerebral connection. In other words, you're unconsciously excluding- or creation separation and disconnection-with the people who aren't attuned to your heightened emotional and feeling-centred frequency. As a feeling type, you need to work on developing honesty with both yourself and others. Being truthful is something that can help you further your goals and connect with others, further forming authentic and deep bonds. Impressing people comes naturally to you, yet too much of it leads to the narcissistic personality disorder mentioned earlier. Egotistical tendencies are ultimately overcome and released by meditation and spiritual practices; therapy, spiritual retreats, healing and shamanic practices. Nature can teach you the lesson of humility combined with greatness.

Just look at nature… the trees stand strong and tall, rooted and powerful. They remind us of the divine simplicity of life and creation itself. The waters of the earth, the rivers, oceans and seas teach us the depth of emotion and of spirit, how everything is interconnected and life is eternal. There is unlimited potential to be found in nature in addition to the realization of your eternal nature. Looking up at the stars and planets at night helps to show you the infinite space available for creation, and how ancient and timeless our souls truly are. Any one of these things observed correctly provide insight into our magnificence. But, nature is humble. It recognizes the healthy flow of giving and receiving energy, and the concept of "interconnectedness." Oneness. This is where divine grace is present. This is something you need to learn and master. Think back to the unhealthy levels of development: you can become exploitative, opportunistic and superior; deceptive, jealous of others or vindictive, and too obsessed on succeeding. Nature's capacity to teach humility and divine simplicity will save you from this.

You can use these revelations for your success too. You don't have to close yourself off to greatness, your main problem lies in how you choose to present yourself- and the attention you seek- when you act from your ego and not your heart space or higher self. Find ways to connect with and align to your higher self. This is the higher mind where divine energy and cosmic consciousness flows. Also, intuition, spiritual and subtle awareness. Meditation brings you back to your heart and higher self and further increases self-awareness, presence, and your inner light. Meditate on authenticity, honesty and truth. You should also participate in charity and humanitarian or environmental projects. Give back to your local communities! Charity work raises your inner vibration while amplifying selflessness within, which, in turn, naturally reduces selfish and egotistical tendencies. A little bit of selfless service goes a long way. In addition to becoming active in your community or local communities through charity service, make a conscious effort to connect with people you love. Spend more time with grandparents, family and close friends- do kind gestures or simply show your appreciation. This takes the attention away from your career and achievements and energizes interpersonal relationships in your life. You might want to consider performing a 'gratitude mantra' daily too.

Finally, take regular breaks, balance work, rest and play. Rest and rejuvenation are extremely important for your mental, emotional, physical and spiritual health. You like to burn the candle at both ends, keep busy, and push yourself. Yet, this isn't healthy and often has the opposite effect of intentions projected. Emotional bonds and real connections can be developed and maintained when you do this, not to mention faithfulness and trust as two essential qualities that will increase. Reflect and write down your follies. Make conscious steps to overcome them; small or major, every step taken towards self-mastery will have powerful results in your personal life. You are a force of change so commit to making change and embracing the darker aspects of your personality, which ultimately lead to your light.

Type 4

Re-cap of key Shadow Traits to overcome:-

- Extreme sensitivities and overly emotional, with a loss of self; vulnerable.
- You're a hopeless romantic, a lone wolf, isolation prone, and cut off from society.
- Too introspective, suffering from low moods and depression, melancholy and darkness.
- Prone too low self-worth and self-esteem when spent too much time in isolation.
- Close relationships suffer and creativity, talents and inspiration demise.

Sensitivity and over-emotionalism are obviously your worst traits which lead to many other minor flaws. You feel things extremely deeply, you're instinctive and intuitive, romantic and "deep." Alchemize your lone wolf tendencies. Instead of feeling like your passions, interests, talents and desires are things you can only do alone, find channels and pathways with like-minded individuals. There are many kindred spirits and soulmates- platonic and romantic- on your wavelength. The first step to wholeness is recognizing this. In fact, you will be surprised at just how many empaths and sensitive people there are in the world. So many people feel the way you do, experience reality in a way similar to your own, and share in your beliefs & values. Lots! Support is all around you. Do you like tarot? Tarot cards are something you should have in your personal tool kit. Spiritual healing, meditation, creative visualization, and nature therapy are other sure routes to personal transformation, in fact these are ideal for you. Type 4s are naturally spiritual even if they don't identify as being spiritual. This is because senstiivty, introversion and self-awareness are key characteristics of being spiritual. Engaging spirituality and healing into daily life is a sure step towards healing and wholeness.

You need to spend time around people as well. Escape your comfort zone. Do this and you will see how it's actually a cage and a shell, not a healthy space. We are inherently social creatures, we naturally seek out paths of family and community. Community ties lead to the best personal growth for you. Volunteering on work exchange places like helping children, land or eco projects, or any other community type organization where you work, live and coexist with other souls wanting to be of service, is ideal for you. You will discover yourself in these environments. Travel is an amazing way to connect to your soul and overcome isolation in the process. Broaden your horizons, experience new cultures, and take regular trips or short breaks. Nature, cities and volunteering are all advised. A key piece of advice for you is to feel the fear and do it anyway. *Now is always the perfect time*. Take that step whether you feel ready, not ready, scared, not scared, secure, insecure, or a mixture of everything! One small step is all it takes. Remember there is never a right mood with you. Your emotional body will always convince you out of something, it's just the way you're wired. Develop fearlessness and courage through working with the fire element. Meditate observing candles, sun gaze, spend time in the shine, and work on strengthening your inner chi. Martial arts are really good for you. Tai chi, kundalini yoga, chi kung/qi gong, aikido and more combative forms of martial art should be practiced. These are highly recommended.

Work on strengthening your logical and intuitive mind. When you do this, you will realize that, 1. You are more than your feelings... Your feelings aren't always your best friend or your true source of inspiration and power. 2. Life is a balance of analytical and logical, reasonable and rational thinking, and intuitive guidance. Instincts and intuition are different things. Instincts arise from your emotional centre, your body and 'inner animal.' They are connected to survival needs and are primal, in essence, and also rooted in desires for emotional connection and bonding. Intuition arises from your higher mind- the higher self. Intuition is your inner guiding light, and although is linked to instinctual responses it is more aligned to the divine; a spiritual and "higher consciousness" perspective. Think of instincts as the body, and gut and intuition as the heart and higher self/mind.

Seek to separate fantasy and illusion from reality too. You have some amazing perspectives and insights into the universe. But, it is easy to get lost in fantasy land or make-believe. Channel this into artistic and imaginative, musical or creative pursuits, by all means, just don't get lost in it. Grounding is useful for you. Ground your energy with the earth by walking bear foot. Hug a tree, even, and work with flower remedies and essential oils. Grow your own herbs and plants, vegetables and crops, or simply spend as much time as possible in the great outdoors. Nature is deeply healing and restorative for you. Crystals and gemstones help to ground your energies as well, so consider learning about Crystal healing and how to use special gemstones to become more rooted. To start, Smoky Quartz, Hematite and Carnelian are perfect options for you. Smoky Quartz dispels fear, negativity and anxiety. It protects you against harmful and negative energy while reducing stress, depression and heavy emotions. Smoky quartz is excellent for emotional calmness, balance and clarity. Hematite is grounding, protecting and physically strengthening. It increases courage, vitality, strength, and yin and yang balance- it balances your yin and yang energies. It dissolves negativity and prevents negative energy absorption, such as harmful intentions or projections from others. Both smoky quartz and hematite are great for your Root chakra. Carnelian is perfect for your Sacral, it boosts fertility, creativity and sexuality and increases libido and self-expression. It is a gemstone for pleasure, the positive path of joy and pleasure. Carnelian alleviates depression and low moods while balancing, stabilizing and harmonizing emotions. Libido and creative life force are both amplified.

Finally, small routines really benefit you and your nature. Create a vision board and a daily routine plan. Tend to the small things, watering your plants, eating healthy, exercising, going for walks, commiting to changing your bank account and financial situation, and tending to your room. Basic hygiene and cleanliness like cleaning your room or home, and helping parents or guardians can help you to find comfort in the physical world, further feeling safe and secure in material reality. You may be surprised at how much a practical or physical routine helps. Self-discipline allows for greater self-awareness and a connection to both your body and environments you reside in. As a 'Heart' enneatype you're primarily concerned with dreams, emotions, memories and your "inner" life. Bodily sensations and physical health can be worked on. And, if you feel yourself drifting away too regularly into the dreamworlds, and daydreaming and getting lost in your imagination for that matter, make a conscious effort to disconnect from this. Cut it out before it becomes too extreme. Balance is required in your life to appreciate your gifts and strengths.

Type 5

Re-cap of key Shadow Traits to overcome:-

- Secretive, isolated, detached… not enough connection, sensual play and expression, and human intimacy.
- Too thoughtful (thinking) and not connected to your feelings or emotions and internal needs.
- Lack of vulnerability, emotional openness and trust.
- Primary fear of being seen as useless or incompetent can lead to insecurity.

As a thinking type, you tend to think quite a lot. Most of your problems arise from overthinking, and you also have an issue with feeling. Staying connected to your body and physical essence is a key way to heal and empower yourself. Your mental abilities and capacity for psychological mastery can be extraordinary, but only when you can integrate other aspects of being and self. Unwinding is a real issue for you. You are rather high-strung and intense, engaging and pure and liberated relaxation is not on your daily or even weekly agenda. This leads to burn-out, stress, and unnecessary tension in your relationships. So, combine the words "therapy" and "self-healing" into your vocabulary. Take time on a cyclic, regular basis (daily, weekly, monthly) to express yourself through music, art, writing and journaling, meditation, or gardening. Cooking with music is a great way to keep you grounded while energizing your mental skills. Cooking is arguably the perfect balance you need, as it allows you to get in tune with your body, physical senses and emotions. The other activities, art and music therapy, writing, and gardening or similar things, are also ideal, however they simultaneously allow you to *introspect*. Being so cerebral means you embody a lot of masculine and 'mind-based' energy. Masculine energy relates to fire and air while the water and earth elements are feminine in nature.

Integrating "yin and yang" theory and some real-world applications that accompany it are linked to this. It is advised that you work on connecting with your feminine nature. This is mainly because earth and water- the qualities and elements you lack- are yin and feminine. If you're a water or earth sign you already have an advantage; you can learn about your astrology star sign to discover what you have a natural affinity with. For example, if you're a type 5 water sign you will naturally feel a resonance with the sea, bodies of water, and the subconscious mind. You could therefore start to pay attention to your dreams, mediate and introspect more, and reflect around lakes, rivers, ponds and oceans. Or, take a long bath with essential oils and some soothing, soul-nourishing or acoustic and jazz music. Anything that enables you to feel and connect to your inner world, the world of emotions, feelings, subtle impression and the "inner you," will help you greatly. If you find out you're an earth sign, you may want to consider grounding and working with the earth, special gemstones and crystals, flower essences and plant and herb remedies. Make your own herbal tinctures, keep crystals around your home, and grow your own vegetables. Walking barefoot on the earth is a powerful way to ground your energies too. Basically, play to your strengths. Your star sign influences your natural likes, dislikes and talents, what comes easily to you and wisdom or knowledge you know instinctively, and what you may need to work on.

Feminine energy is also associated with the 'Heart' centre, one of the three main centres as taught by the Enneagram that you're lacking in. As a 'Head' type your gifts lie in cerebral and mental abilities. You interact with others through fine-tuned observation skills, but you're not very instinctive or emotionally intelligent, empathic and intuitive. Stay connected to your body so energy can flow properly and effectively. If ever in doubt, remember that you are a holistic being. You're supposed to energize all parts of you, instincts relating to the body included. Jog, dance, move more, do yoga, work out, and engage in sports of movement for pleasure. This releases positive hormones that lead to joy and positivity. Being high-strung means you must relax, let go and have fun, and movement is a key way to move trapped emotions and stored/blocked trauma. In addition, meditation and yoga are extremely helpful for your type, because *mental blocks* can be released. Memories can be sparked (as associated with your heart and feelings) and intuition can be developed. As you have issues with feeling intellectually superior it would be wise to regularly seek expert advice- sage counsel and guidance from an elder, sensei or master, or well-respected expert in their field. It doesn't matter what path you go through- tarot, a Reiki Master, a Shaman, seer or clairvoyant, astrologer or business mentor.. just seek advice. This strengthens and empowers your

165

'humility muscle.' Going to one of these on a regular & cyclic basis enables you to humble yourself and continue to learn and grow, with grace and modesty.

To overcome loneliness, mistrust and isolation, form a few close intimate relationships. Maybe you feel the way you do because you've been misled? In such an extroverted society there's a lot of emphasis on social get-togethers, parties and knowing lots of people. Yet you are suited to a few intimate friendships. Make a conscious effort to open up emotionally and trust others with your feelings, beliefs, and stories. At your best you're an open-minded, pioneering visionary with skilled mastery, so find the people you resonate with and feel an affinity with and keep them close. You might want to consider redefining your belief system around conflict and confrontation too. It's natural for conflicts to arise- conflict and chaos paves the way for unity, harmony and connections. Instead of blocking off attachments because of fear of conflict or being hurt, re-define what you deem 'acceptable.' Inner strength, integrity and character develop form disagreements and opportunities for finding balance. Despite the apparently contradictory information presented earlier, work on developing your inner yang and masculine energy purely in terms of assertiveness. Air energy linked to cerebral and intellectual gifts may be masculine, however you still need to master self-assertion and the inner fire needed for conflict resolution. Isolation can turn into escapism, otherwise! Ask your dreams for guidance. Your subconscious mind is readily available to assist you.

Type 6

Re-cap of key Shadow Traits to overcome:-

- Anxious, suspicious, worrisome and negative. Indecisive and procrastinating.
- Lack of self-care, defensive, and weak boundaries.
- So wrapped up in intimate connections and depth of human spirit that you lose yourself.
- Playing victim, being offended and self-delusion.
- Insecurity leading to rebellious and defiant tendencies and behaviors.

As a cerebral and thinking type your main issue is in your inability to connect to your instincts. Instinctual responses and intuition suffer greatly as a result. You're loyal and considerate, yet you question yourself frequently. You also feel persecuted, judged, defenseless, and irrational; you believe people are out to get you and that you will be punished or vindicated. This all arises from lack of self-esteem and feelings of inferiority. So, the best thing you could do is to work on connecting to your body, instincts, and dreams. The inner realms of subtle impressions, feelings, moods, emotions and extrasensory gifts arising from feminine, introspective and yin energies are where you would be best to focus your attention on. Society has conditioned us to believe being shy, reserved or introverted are 'weird,' or symbolic of solely being an arty or distant type. But this isn't the case. Yin and yang are the fundamental forces of life- they complement each other, they flow into one another... Yin flows into yang and yang back into yin. Yin energy is receptive, passive, feminine and magnetic, whilst yang is active, dominant, masculine and electric. Yin relates to emotions and the body and yang is symbolic of the mind and intellect, which includes rationality, reason & logic. Thus, you possess many qualities of 'yin,' being so caring and loyal, affectionate and the like, however you are predominantly "mental" (thinking/in your mind). This essentially means you rationalize your feelings out of existence! And this leads to illusion, ambiguity and false evidence appearing real: fear.

If a star sign were to be assigned to this enneatype it would be the zodiac sign *Virgo* (and we explore this connection in the next book to this Enneagram series). Everyone suffers from anxiety from time to time, yet to beat yourself up for it isn't healthy. It leads to a number of health issues and tension and discord in relationships. Be more present and compassionate with your anxious tendencies. Treat yourself with the same care and patience as you would others. Explore it, even- journal, express your worries and follies through art music, poetry, drawing and dance. Let your body, mind and emotions flow. Work creatively with your stresses and tensions, don't turn to alcohol or substance, and be honest with yourself. Self-honesty is key for you. Calming herbal teas are ideal for you... Drink chamomile tea before sleep and at regular times throughout the day. Passionflower, valerian root and lemon balm are other soothing and calming tea choices. Try to substitute sugar for natural sweetener, organic and ethical honey, or even fairtrade brown sugar. When alchemized anxiety can be transformed into excitement and a positive type of inner fire, almost acting a kind of "tonic." This comes back to shifting your mindset and committing to self-help and positivity. Spending more time in the sunshine is equally stimulating and empowering- sunshine or solar energy is a life force, it's dominant, empowering and increases self-esteem. It inspires optimism and a positive, healthy & self-assertive mindset.

Self-therapy in the form of meditation, mantras and affirmations, neurolingusitic programming, and other forms of "brain training"- rewiring your brain and neurological patterns will help you considerably throughout life. You would benefit from listening to binaural beats and isochronic tones daily. These allow you to explore your emotions, beliefs and inner world, in addition to accessing the subconscious realm and mind, while positively altering thought and mental patterns. Binaural beats essentially rewire your brain and raise your frequency, expand your aura/electromagnetic biofield, and contribute to optimistic thinking and calm, balanced and harmonized emotions. The moment binaural beats are received by your brain healing (to make whole) begins. Faulty perceptions and internal distortions of the mind and emotional body start to become unraveled, and you feel lighter, more positive, inspired and future thinking. People who listen to binaural beats frequently are generally quite content and optimistic. They don't dwell on the past or get stuck there, so they're able to look towards their future (and be content and mindful in the present) with a sense of vitality, passion and enthusiasm.

Because stress and nervous tension is caused by bad diet and lifestyle choices, you would be best off making physical changes. You're not very connected to your emotions, inner realm of feelings and memories, or instincts, therefore changing diet will provide the energy and life force you need. Remember that mind, body & spirit are connected; moving your physical body and treating it right with nutritious and healthy foods allows emotions to flow. And, your mind can be programmed to a better, ascended and higher frequency. The Higher Self is the opposite of the lower self- a lot of your fears and irrational worries stem from disconnection with your higher self. So, adopt a holistic approach to healing. Heal your emotions and body to heal your mind and vice versa. You function best with wholefoods and a plant based, sugar and carb free diet. Because you struggle most with nervous tension as linked to the nervous system, try to cut out excess carbs, all processed and artificial foods, and sugar. Eat as many nuts, seeds, vegetables, fruits, wholegrains and wheats, legumes, pulses and lean and clean proteins. Holistic movements like taichi, chi kung and yoga would equally benefit you. If the gym of traditional sports isn't for you take regular walks in nature, in your local park or nature reserve, or beach or forest. Dance for pleasure too, just be active! But don't see it as a chore as this will only add to your stress levels; instead be active to experience pleasure and emotional satisfaction. Think in terms of joy and happiness and the emotional and psychological release that happens during movement.

Finally, pay attention to your dreams. Self-reflection and 'going within' to make sense of things is very, very helpful for you. Past memories, experiences and emotions are a route to your true self, back to source and centre. Self-therapy (art, music, meditation) and journaling are key activities for you to consciously make time for. A dream diary or journal will assist you in coming to terms with your "follies," your shadow self and personality traits. Everything considered dark, worthy of denial or repression- or outright rejection- are things you should spend some time evaluating. Denial gives rise to more of what we don't want (*what we resist, persists*) and this is the case with your personality type. Dreams are a powerful path to self-discovery, finding balance within, and integrating the light and dark parts of your psyche and self. Depending on your star sign you could very well have 'visionary powers;'psychic and precognitive/clairvoyant gifts linking to prophetic dreams. If this is the case, you should certainly be looking towards your astrological make-up as defined in your birth/natal chart to help to ease the more 'Head' based characteristics of your enneatype. Logic and reason can transform significantly into reaching out and connecting with others on a more engaging, authentic, and warm level. This simultaneously helps you to develop trust.

Type 7

Re-cap of key Shadow Traits to overcome:-

- Distracted, restless, unfocused, uncommitted and self-absorbed.
- Lacking focus and direction, commitment and stability.
- Frivolous and unfaithful- you can dismiss people and projects in a heartbeat.
- Impulsive, undisciplined, impatient and brash; over-enthusiastic.

This is a very fiery and impulsive personality type, so it may be quite obvious what you need to do to calm such an excitable and spontaneous character. If you're familiar with astrology you will know that personality type 7 could very well read as the Sagittarius star sign, so seek to embody more water and earth energy in your life. Water is sensitive, receptive, magnetic and empathic. Water interacts on an emotional and sincere level, helping to ease some of the superificality associated with being so impulsive and extroverted. Water is also yin or feminine in nature while type 7 is a 'Head' enneatype, thus being primarily focused on mental activities. Pursuits, passions and personality characteristics are masculine, in essence. Therefore, the water element can be worked with and embodied

173

for a more holistic and balanced lifestyle. Spend time near bodies of water; lakes, rivers and oceans, to feel more connected to your inner world of impressions and emotions. It's not that you're unemotional, it's just that you're always on the go and seeking the next best experience. This leads to shallowness and frivolity. Water energy will help to give a gentle steam to your fire and self-awareness, empathy and gentleness to your airy mental nature. Keep a check on your impatience and impulsions- don't' feed them, however make a mental note to be more conscious and honest with the things that 'fuel your fire.' Fire and passion are great, just not to the extent you show them. For example, relationships and commitments often suffer as a direct result; you sacrifice things, people and projects too easily.

Create a vision board of your future self. Imagine you are your future self, some point later in life... how would you want to see yourself, looking back? Wouldn't you have wanted to create something, expand through a job and reach new heights in your career? Or, would you have wanted to have stuck at that relationship, grow and evolve together to learn lots of significant life lessons? Or perhaps have given birth to (created) children, a home and strong foundation, a family or lasting career with longevity? Thinking and 'projecting' yourself into the future can help put things into perspective. A vision board can literally serve as a vision for a future projection of your ultimate life. Dreams, aspiration and goals are supposed to be followed through- not just glimpsed and given a little bit of time and energy to before reneging. Also, meditate on patience. Cultivate as much patience and empathy as you can through meditation and mindful practices. Being so impulsive means you lack empathy, more so than you would like to admit! You lack the depth and feeling necessary for lasting bonds. Look towards the attributes of the 'Heart' centre where memories, emotions and feelings are strong. Dreams and your inner life can provide the answers and self-awareness you seek. Oh yes, unlike the previous two enneatypes who also belong to the 'Head' category, being so enthusiastic and liberated means you're on a lifelong journey of self-discovery, which signifies that you're deeply philosophical. You're open to learning, and you're happy to learn, absorb and exchange information and ideas. The "inner you" is part of this self-discovery.

So, meditation and different types of introspective and introverted therapy can really help you. The imagination, music, art and self-expression can really allow you to get in tune with the inner you, and this naturally helps you to slow down and connect with your higher mind/self. Sublime expressions of the soul satisfy your need for excitement and movement just as they help connect to the subtle energies available. Any route or pathway to spiritual alignment, the soul, psyche, subconscious and universal archetypes or esoteric wisdom are ideal for you. Subtle energy is an integral part of life and self, yet you don't access it as much as you could because you're always on the go. Movement is very 'yang' in nature. Stillness and silence are yin… Be more mindful of the subtle and spiritual energies at play and how there are multiple dimensions. Instead of sticking to the tried and tested, i.e. being enthusiastic and full of life force and vitality, moving and seeking new things and experience, try and look within to see without. There are worlds and galaxies within you, in your mind, heart, psyche and spirit. Self-therapy, dreaming, meditation and divine expressions through art, music and the like are perfect ways to achieve self-realization.

Going back to being so yang and masculine, in addition to water 'earth' will help to ground you. Earth energy is receptive and introverted, 'yin' in nature and quite simply the opposite of both fire and air. Grounding is an essential self-development tool. Ground by walking barefoot on earth, hugging trees, contemplating or mediating in nature, and incorporating earth element activities into your life. Garden, start your own herb or vegetable garden, and look into flower essences or herbal remedies. Plants, crystals and gemstones are all connected to earth energy and the earth element, thus these are highly recommended. Consider taking a course in Nutrition or Herbal Medicine, or going once or twice a year to work on an organic farm, eco-community, or permaculture placement for a few weeks or months. The latter options will please your desires for travel and adventure while strengthening your capacity for commitment and responsibility equally. Qualities of earth include duty, security, responsibility, and practicalities. Serenity and grace come with both water and earth, and instincts and intuition increase simultaneously. Intuition serves as our guiding light and can aid in overcoming the more brash aspects of your personality. And, instincts are amplified and developed when you move away from such a logical and planning ahead mindset, and start to become more present. Live in the now. Become aware of your body, surroundings, environments and feelings in the present moment. Soul-searching and self-growth tie into this.

Overall, you just need to commit to making changes to embody more serenity, grace and self-awareness. Get in tune with your feelings, inner moods and dreams (through water energy) and connect to your body and physical world (through earth energy). Develop your listening skills as well. Refrain from talking excessively. Cut down external stimulation and distractions like t.v.constant background music or noise. Silence should be your new best friend! Finding comfort in silence allows you to feel content in your own being. Also, try to overcome instant gratification, always wanting everything now. There so much that can be achieved in the present moment, so many sensations and endless wisdom and knowledge to be found. You never know what could spark when you learn to be more present, self-aware, and mindful. Aim for quality over quantity.

Type 8

Re-cap of key Shadow Traits to overcome:-

- Domineering, controlling and intimidating; overpowering.
- Confrontational, temperamental and combative.
- Cold and callous, emotionally disconnected, lacking sensitivity and heart.
- Dictatorial and delusions of invisibility or greatness.

As a type 8, you are deeply instinctive. You certainly don't have a problem expressing yourself in an empowered and self-assertive way. But, you can be disconnected from empathy, emotions and senstiivty- you can be overpowering and even tyrannical or dictatorial at times. The best thing you could do, therefore, is to work on your emotional empathy and sensitivity; your water, yin and feminine qualities. Connecting to the water element will help you to show self-restraint. It naturally calms your burning inner fire and assertiveness, amplifies your desire for peace and compromise, and eases aggressive or confrontational feelings you may experience. Water is adaptable, receptive and subtly powerful- it 'goes with the flow' without being in your face or arrogant. There is a humble and modest quality about water, yet this doesn't mean it isn't powerful; people with a lot of water energy in their natal chart or constitution have a unique personal magnetism. They're aware that real change comes about through connection. I.e. not seeking to gain control or implement change through pushing someone else down, quietning them, or suppressing their views and beliefs. Water is instead flexible and all-embracing, it's accepting, tolerant and non-judgemental- not to mention patient.

Working with the water element also allows your instincts to shine and thrive. It doesn't suppress instinctive responses and your direct approach , as you may initially believe. The key for you is to recondition your mind into no longer thinking water (and it's qualities and associations) are weak. Passivity, gentleness and humility are not weaknesses. Kindness, adaptability and silent power aren't weaknesses either. Being so instinctual has many positive qualities. Yet, instincts imply dominance and unconscious responses, they are our triggers and ego defences- more so for you than any other enneatype. There's a magic to water (as opposed to fire, your ruling quality). Celestial vibrations can hit you in the most magical, empowering, and healing ways if you allow yourself to change and adapt. What does this mean practically? Learn to let go and ease control. Be open to listening to others, and learning from them, while reminding yourself daily of the motivations behind your inspiration. Seeking inspiration and stepping into self-leaderships is birthed from pure motives. So, why allow the more negative aspects of your persona to take over? Self-acceptance followed by openness to change are two key steps for you. True power is not exerting force or dominance when you know you can... True power is further being cooperative, kind and encouraging instead of limiting others through your strong beliefs and action-focused demeanour.

Consider spending time every week or month volunteering with animals or the elderly. Anyone who is at a disadvantage, disabled or in need of care and help, give your time to them. Small acts of kindness amplify your personal vibration, so you start to feel more compassionate and generous. Help animals in need or even become an elderly companion- observe how joy and gratitude expands in your life. Raw emotions are the doorway to self-development, and you're definitely capable of deep and authentic emotions. Your instincts will tell you to care, nurture and protect, so sometimes it really is as simply as entering an environment- creating the possibility and space- for love amplification. Unconditional love for others is tied into self-love too. The more loving and genuinely caring we are towards others the more we feel drawn to engage in self-love and self-care, and vice versa. This then further allows you to transcend your tendency of alienating those closest to you. It's a sort of self-perpetuating prophecy: you think people are against you, or aren't happy for you, due to your own self-doubts and internal projections (manifested from instincts, a 'survival' mindset) however this isn't necessarily the case. Make a conscious effort to remind people of your love for them. Be more affectionate and supportive of their dreams and goals, and their success and achievements regardless of how minor. Ironically, you depend on many people although you give off the image of being self-reliant. This is one of your main if not most major self-delusions. Codependency is a shadow aspect of this enneatype, despite how strong and independent you are and like to believe.

Strive for real independence by not needing to bring others down or question their path to validate yours. Flexibility should be cultivated as should non-judgement. Learn to be more tolerant and unconditionally accepting, as your self-sufficiency is largely an illusion. And, you overvalue power and prestige, success and fame or prosperity. In the same breath you undervalue emotional connection, friendship, family bonds and sensitive exchanges and affections. Warmth is something you can expand through releasing control, hugging the people you love more, and smiling. Smile, dance in the rain or great outdoors, sing and observe birds inapark. Did you know bird song is one of the quickest stress relievers?! Simply sitting on the ground by a tree or on a bench, observing and listening to nature including birds singing will instantly help you feel more connected. Look after your emotional, psychological, and spiritual health. Being a 'Gut' centre means you're naturally instinctive, as already mentioned, but other aspects of you are important to take care of too. Health is holistic, you are a holistic person. So evaluate what makes you happy and brings you joy. Perhaps you need more intimacy and human affection both romantic or sexual and platonic.... Maybe you're seeing so much negativity and separation in your life because you've forgotten the power and importance of liberated, fun and blissfully euphoric play… Let your inner child shine and run wild. Being free to express yourself creatively, imaginatively, sensually, sexually and innocently will remove blocked emotions, wounds and faulty perceptions or belief systems. Movement is a *medicine*. Speaking of medicine, music, art and nature therapy are all healers and you should incorporate self-healing or therapy into your life. No-one is above music or meditation. Spiritual and shamanic healing would be great for you as they open gateways to the spiritual and subtle worlds, and move your focus away from the materialistic world. In the materialistic VS spiritual balance you don't seem to be too spiritually open or aware. Yet, you have visionary qualities. Connect to the divine and your intuition on a daily basis; star-gaze, moon-gaze and sun-gaze- watch the stars at night, and spend lots of time in nature. Anything that aids in returning you back to your natural state of being, your organic state and self, will work wonders.

Type 9

Re-cap of key Shadow Traits to overcome:-

- Self-sacrificing, appeasing and apathetic.
- Tunes out reality, inability to say no; peace at any price.
- Loneliness, anxiety, depression, lack of self-awareness and repressions.

As the Peacemaker your main problem in life is becoming a pushover; people-pleasing, appeasing and self-sacrificing. You lack fire- the self-assertion and self-confidence to stand your ground. You don't have a problem sticking up for people you love- or even complete strangers, but you don't give yourself the same love and care. You do what others want and say to be 'nice.' You lack boundaries and have a very hard time saying 'no' too. So, increasing your inner fire will help you greatly. You need to work on your yang, the fiery, active and masculine energy that is opposite to yin. You're naturally yin aka passive in nature, yet this leaves you open to misfortune and satisfaction. Increasing your inner yang can be done in a number of ways. Firstly, spend more time in the sunshine. Solar energy is incredibly empowering; it aids in increasing vitality and personal passions, you feel more connected to personal aspirations, goals &

dreams. Solar energy is also a confidence and self-esteem booster. Have you heard of sun-gazing? Sun-gazing is staring at the sun around 45 minutes after it rises and the same amount of time before it sets. You should do this in a meditative and contemplative way... Sun-gazing is excellent for your pineal gland, the gland in your brain responsible for light absorption and important circadian rhythms (like the sleep-wake cycle). The pineal gland benefits considerably from sun-gazing and sun-gazing is a technique believed to be performed by the ancients, such as ancient Egyptians, Indians and Greeks.

In addition to the sun energizing your passions and aspirations it can also enhance communication. This is because solar energy is assertive, active and forceful (dominant), therefore it stimulates meridians and energy pathways within. This "forcefulness" enables you to pay attention to what is going on within and around, it allows you to exert yourself. Passivity transforms into action and receptivity into a type of electric dominance. You need to be more of an active participant in your life. This may seem contradictory as your centre is the 'Gut,' the body and instinctive centre, thus advice given to the other enneatypes is contrary; others should seek to embody characteristics from the other centres (Head and Heart). However, although you are ruled by instincts you don't possess the direct approach the other Gut personality types do. You treat your life almost as a bystander or onlooker, when at your lowest. Make peace with your follies to overcome this. Tuning things out because they appear too aggressive or chaotic, combative or conflicting for you doesn't help you nor does it serve your higher self. You must learn how to accept and embrace the 'dark' or tricky parts of the human nature. In other words, do some shadow work healing and integration! Introspect, dream, journal, meditate and initiate paths to healing and wholeness that are in alignment with shadow acceptance.

We all have a shadow self…. There's also the collective shadow and our individual shadow selves, the individual shadow being the traits and flaws that are specific to our enneatype, sun sign, moon sign, life path and the like. You're lucky as yours are quite obvious, it's just a case of coming to terms with them and no longer pushing them below the surface. Don't deny, reject or repress. The only way up and out is through, you must go into the pain and discomfort to rise. Connection is important to you therefore it is essential that you learn how to do this. Becoming mentally and emotionally engaged with the world around are things you can seek to master. Work on strengthening your *subtle muscles*, i.e. self-talk (mental muscle) and the way you respond to people and situations (emotional muscles). You have anxieties, aggressions and other feelings you consider "lower" or "impure." Negative sensations, feelings and thoughts are a core part of existence, yin flows into yang just as yang flows back into yin. Together they create unity. Yin is darkness, it is linked to the moon and the subconscious and therefore the shadow self. In addition to sun gazing and being in sunshine to increase the masculine qualities of assertiveness and action, you should also consider the effect the moon's rays have on you. Everything associated with darkness and the shadow realms can be meditation on for comprehension. Journal to find out past feelings and memories associated with undesirable, or uncomfortable, experiences. Express yourself artistically and imaginatively- these are perfect for your psyche and emotional body.

Art, music, dance, journalling, nature therapy, yoga, martial arts, and any creative activity will let the inner you come out to play, heal and shine. Whatever feels right, just be free! Let your instincts out, as you have a primal and animal side even if you don't want to admit it. This is another thing… Primality, sexuality and sensuality, and creativity are intrinsically connected to the Higher Self and mind, and your spiritual body. If you know anything about Chakra philosophy you will be aware that the kundalini; one's serpent-power that flows through an active and balanced chakra system, is representative of sexual (also sensual), psychic (also spiritual) and creative (also imaginative) energy. They're a trinity. Each influences one another and blocks in any one of these areas will negatively affect the others, just as vibrancy and a free flow of energy positively empowers the others. Accepting your "inner animal" is a strong step towards accepting other parts of your personality- and other people's. Impulses and emotions which feel wrong, impure or alien to you are a different part of yourself speaking out. I'm not referring to murder, rape or vilence, some acts are clearly inhumane and unnatural going against natural law morailty & ethics; this is referring to the urges and desires rooted in primality. Sexual needs, survival needs, desires for intimacy and affection, security and everything related to your lower chakras- the root and sacral- come in here. Make peace with yourself in order to step into the best version of yourself, the Peacemaker.

Self-awareness can be improved with energy healing and seeing a Reiki Master, shaman or other practitioner of the Healing Arts. Edlers, mentors, therapists and healers will assist in self-discovery, evaluating your past and conflicts, and further your contribution in relationship issues. Your feelings for others are wrapped into your identity and self-esteem so this can be difficult for you, but it is more than worth it in the end. Seeking professionals and experienced healers and helpers also open you up to the mysteries of the universe, or simply expert knowledge that can lead to self-realization. Wisdom should be a goal of yours as wisdom births awareness. And, sometimes the path to peace is not peaceful. Conflict and disagreement is honest and real and is occasionally/often necessary for long-term peace. In other words, you need to accept your inner darkness and personal karma, even if it's negative, to evolve through to the light. Long-term peace, happiness and victory far outweighs any short-term or momentary 'superficial peace.' Your key to self-development is all about being real with yourself. Meditate on (envision) genuine relationships characterized by deep and loving bonds. Picture your future self surrounded by authentic friends, family and a community of loving and supportive souls. A vision board would be a beautiful way to intentionally create your future and energize it daily. Finally, next to spiritual healing and therapy consider a holistic exercise regime or sport, something that works on the psychological/mental, emotional, physical and spiritual planes. Regular exercise increases self-discipline, helps you to stay connected to your instincts, fine-tunes your emotions, and sparks healing on multiple levels. Movement also serves as a medicine to your mind and soul while aiding in the development of body-awareness. Of course, exercise allows for the release of aggression, tension and built up frustrations!

Balancing Your 3 Main Centres

One concept we haven't explored yet is the centres. The Enneagram teaches that there are three main centres: the Head, the Heart and the Gut. This is interesting, as if you're familiar with Chakra and Yogic philosophy, you will know that there are significant chakra points that influence us more powerfully than others. These are the Sacral, the centre of emotions, creativity and sexuality; the heart, the centre of love and empathy and a bridge between the lower self and higher self (and lower consciousness & higher consciousness); and the third eye, the seat of all spiritual insight and psychic phenomena, including intuition, perceptiveness, and an ability to perceive from your higher self. It tends to be that blocks and distortions in these three centres cause the most damage on the mental, emotional, physical and spiritual planes, and vice versa; i.e. the more we heal them the more empowered we become. Being familiar with Chakras, you will also know that the Enneagram's interpretation of the 3 significant centres corresponds perfectly to the third eye (Head), heart (Heart), and sacral (Gut) chakras.

So, the **Head** is where we process information. It has intrinsic links to the mind and mental process, or intellect, and relates to Personality types 5, 6 and 7. Problem-solving, thinking, imagination, planning, memory, intellectual pursuits, perception and information-gathering all come under the Head centre's realm. The Head is the *thinking* centre.

The **Heart** is where we process information through feelings and relates to relationships with self and others, self-expression, emotions and connections. Personality types 2, 3 and 4 tie into the Heart centre. The Heart is the *feeling* centre.

The **Body or Gut** links to our intuition, instinctual responses and gut-feelings. Personality types 8, 9 and 1 relate to the Gut/Body centre, which is the *instinctive* centre.

In addition to learning about your Enneatype, Holy Idea, Virtue, Passion, Ego-Fixation, and strengths and weaknesses, one of the main purposes of Enneagram wisdom is to balance these three centres within. Although each centre relates to 3 specific personality types, this does not mean balance and harmony cannot be attained within. You can learn a great deal about yourself through exploring the other

Enneatypes in relation to their corresponding "centre," even if it isn't your main personality type.

The Body/Gut Centres

Type 8: 8s respond to triggers and emotional issues through anger and in some physical-instinctual way, such as raising their voice, becoming more aggressive and domineering in mannerism, and seeking to exert control and physical authority over others. Lust, their *Passion*, is a physical quality and vengeance, the *Ego-Fixation*, is also manifested and represented as a physical act.

Type 9: 9s also have very instinctual Passions and Ego-Fixations. Slothfulness and laziness/ indolence are both rooted in disconnection from one's divine physical self, and accompanying characteristics and tendencies include denying or repressing anger and natural instinctual shadow traits. In the pursuit of harmony and idealism 9s will deny their instinctual urges and turn away from their whole, balanced and unified self.

Type 1: 1s equally have primarily instinctual responses and inner drives when they lose touch with their true essence. The Ego-Fixation of resentment and the Passion of anger come into play when they are not having their physical needs met, and this further creates tension on a physical level. 1s also attempt to control or repress their anger and inner gut-feelings.

The Heart/Feeling Centres

Type 2: 2s display Passion and Ego-Fixation in harmony with their feelings, thus showing how they are ruled by their corresponding centre. Pride is a representation of losing touch with their strengths regarding their connection to others, and this is often expressed through wanting or getting people to like them. 2s rely on positive emotional experiences and feelings with others. The same as shared for pride is true with flattery.

Type 3: Just like type 2, type 3s are primarily concerned with their connection and interaction with others. Deceit and vanity, the Passion and Ego-Fixation respectively, are birthed from a disconnection with self and their true self, which is always in full force when they have authentic bonds. If 3s are out of tune with their feelings and sincere, authentic and truthful emotions, their virtues are diminished.

Type 4: The envy and melancholy felt by 4s when they lose touch with their essence, Holy Idea and Virtue represent a basic need to feel and be in unity with others. Type 4s are concerned with their individuality, creativity and gifts and talents, and how they can tune into these to inspire or experience deep connections with others. Feeling and authentic human bonds are the keys here.

The Head/Thinking Centres

Type 5: 5s are part of the thinking centre and this is clearly reflected in their traits and tendencies. Avarice (the Passion) and stinginess (the Ego-Fixation) both stem from a mental distortion or imbalance which desires excessive material wealth and prosperity; a lot of desires in the physical realm are birthed from the mind. 5s at their worst become secretive, isolated and emotionally and mentally withdrawn, and at their best are scholarly and perceptive.

Type 6: 6s negative/shadow attributes include fear, cowardice and pessimism, and these all begin in the mind, or in some mental distortion. In their positive self they are problem-solvers, attentive and philosophical, which are again all mind based.

Losing touch with their true self can make them doubtful and anxious- minor mental health issues.

Type 7: Type 7s turn to gluttony (Passion) and planning (Ego-Fixation). The need to constantly plan and forward-think is due to a disconnection with the present moment, with peace of mind in the now; and gluttony does not just relate to food but also an excessive accumulation of beliefs, ideas and perspectives. Sobriety, their Holy Idea, requires calmness of mind and becoming conscious in the present moment.

So, in terms of self- discovery and personal transformation, it may be clear how you can learn about each Personality type to help balance your own inner currents. Just because you resonate with one Personality type it doesn't mean you won't have aspects from the others. Remember that the Ennegaram is only one system of self-discovery and analysis; we also have astrology and other esoteric systems playing integral significance in our personality's make-up. Numerology, for example, shows us how our date of birth and name can be highly important to our growth and self- awareness. In astrology, it is not just our sun sign which affects us deeply but also rising/ ascendent, moon sign and all other planetary placements. Quite simply, the

Enneagram may be a powerful system yet it is just one system- we are complex individuals.

The Gut/Instinctive Centre, In Relation to the Sacral Chakra

The *sacral chakra* is the energetic wheel or portal corresponding to the Gut, or Instinctive and Body centre. The sacral relates to emotions, creativity and sexuality- it can be seen as a trinity and merging of all three. Repressed emotions and past painful memories in friendships, sexual bonds or relationships often store in the sacral chakra. If there is a block in this centre's energy portal, this can cause major issues in relationships and creative expression, and in the way one connects and relates to others. Emotional blocks, imbalances and disharmonious are often manifested in the sacral chakra. In relation to this same spot being the gut and instinctive centre in the Enneagram, the same is true with the chakra system. The sacral is also known as your "gut centre" as it is where instinctual and primal urges and desires come from. We are both spirit and human, therefore we have an animalistic essence to our nature. Primality and passion are two fundamental elements of life, and if we begin to repress or deny them this where problems can arise.

It is interesting to know that a lot of issues with the shadow self and personality take root in some self-denial, largely repressed or rejected part of self, and this usually to almost has its roots in the sacral chakra's energetic associations. Desire, lust, a need for intimacy and connection, and deep emotional longings all link to the sacral and the shadow self equally. When we look at the Enneagram and its teachings, the shadow self (shadow or dark personality traits) and the divine are both integral to Enneagram philosophy. Furthermore, instinctual responses and needs are birthed from our sexuality and desire for human connection. Learning about the sacral chakra can teach us a lot in terms of understanding the nature of the Enneagram and the Gut/ Body centre's Personality types specifically. When the sacral chakra is blocked, i.e. there is no longer a free flow of energy from or through it, this can close one off from their intuition. In chakra philosophy it is believed and taught that the sacral chakra is closely linked to the Third Eye chakra, the seat of vision, psychic ability, perception, connection to the divine and the higher self, and intuition. This "natural cord" or link between sacral (lower self/ primality/ emotions/ sex centre) and the third eye (higher self/ centre for intuition and psychic- spiritual gifts/ perception) provides key insight into how we can balance our Gut and Head centres when using the Enneagram. Quite simply, learning of the energetic associations of these chakras opens up new portals to learning, self-discovery, understanding and transformation.

The Heart, In Relation to the Heart Chakra (Main Centre for Empathy, Love and Relationships)

The heart chakra is actually known as the central chakra is this unique system and this is due to the heart being directly between the higher centres/charas and the lower ones. There are believed to be 7 main chakras, or energy portals, on the human body and these are connected by the heart. The heart chakra symbolizes empathy, unconditional love, caring, kindness, relationships, friendships, a balance between dependency and independence, and a respect and care for nature and the planet, environment and natural world. The heart chakra connects "lower" feelings and emotions, including our basic instinctual urges and desires, and "higher" ones. The main word and quality associated with the heart chakra is empathy and its important to understand the importance of empathy here and how it relates to both the heart chakra and Heart centre in the Enneagram. Once you start to connect to your own inner divinity, internal currents and true soul's purpose, you begin to feel more in tune with yourself. (Your 'self'.) Well, with this naturally comes feeling your inner energy currents and being more open to spirit and subtle energy.

The Head, In relation to the Third Eye and Crown Chakras

Finally, your Head centre is naturally connected to the third eye and crown chakras. Your third eye as briefly discussed is your psychic centre. An open and healthy third eye chakra can lead to the ability to perceive subtle energy, enhanced and evolved intuition, spiritual gifts, access to dream states, intellect, innovation, original thinking, and imaginative qualities and thought process. As it is located just below the crown chakra, it also assists in the free flow of energy from the crown to the root chakra; the base chakra relating to security, grounding and feeling connected to both your own body and the earth. As for your crown chakra specifically the crown is at the top of your head and is known as the seat of cosmic consciousness. Associations include universal truth and wisdom, higher perspectives and understanding, spiritual awareness, mediumship and channeling, and a connection to source, the divine & some higher power. The crown chakra, however, is not exclusive to all things supernatural or spiritual, it is also very much connected to the earth. This is because the energy which flows through all 7 chakras is known as kundalini, or shakti, when awakened, in healthy flow and harmonious, and this flows from crown (all the way at the top) to the root (all the way at the base of the spine, by the pelvic region and reproductive organs).

Why is this necessary to know, you may be wondering? Well if you go back and read Enneagram History and Roots you will be aware that a connection to the divine and *essence* is inherent within many ancient and spiritual traditions and teachings. Your kundalini energy is also known as "serpent power" and has strong ties to the story of Christianity, regarding the snake in the Garden of Eden. The snake as a symbol essentially represents our sexuality, inner divinity and whole, unified and balanced state of being. There is a reason why those may choose to repress or deny their own primal, sensual and sexual urges and nature call this "evil." Dark and light, evil and good, and shadow and dark- the principle is universal and it is furthermore contained in the cells of our very own DNA. Meditation, sound healing, spiritual exercises and self- healing can all help us access the core of our beings and our ancient memories simultaneously, and assist us in understanding our own chakras- as energetic portals stemming back to ancient Sanskrit times.

So regardless of how deep you wish to go into the chakra system and how you choose to integrate it into your understanding and application of the Enneagram, having a basic knowledge and awareness of the following chakras; the *Sacral*, *Heart* and *Third Eye & Crow*n, at the very least, can open new channels for learning and self- discovery, also furthering your understanding of the 3 centres and how to balance them.

Balancing Steps & Guidance

Gut/Body (instincts), Heart (feeling) and Head (thinking) are within each of us regardless of our Personality type. It is advocated that whichever centre our Enneatype resides in is the centre we are *least* able to function, because the psyche naturally has some ego blocks and distortions. For example, type 9 resides in the Body centre, yet type 9's struggle most with feeling connected to their bodies and often lose touch with their inner vitality and physical essence. Integrating all three centres, therefore, is a step towards self- awareness, growth and shifts for change.

To balance the Body/Gut centre….

Remember the power of physical movement. Exercise, dance, and physical movements release trapped emotions and blocks in the subtle energy bodies. Energy pathways needa free flow of energy for healing, growth and personal self-discovery, transformation and self-alignment. We tend to repress painful memories and experiences which ultimately lead to blocks. Trapped energy, unconscious triggers, and unresolved traumas and pain. Movement will instantly help to move these and further release them. Additionally, you should engage in exercise that you actually enjoy. Pleasurable activities stimulate psychological and emotional well-being too, and you are surely aware of the holistic nature of self. The mind, emotions, body and spirit are all designed to work in harmony. Blocks in one will affect the state of health of the others. Joy and pleasure combined with "movement medicine" is exactly that, a medicine. It's healing, restorative and transformational. Also, anything which gets you in tune with your senses. Dance, tai chi, martial arts, sports, walks in nature, kundalini yoga, swimming, making love… all of these can work wonders for your gut and instinctual energies.

Engaging in any physical exercise or activity that connects you to your body, to your senses, naturally releases (eases) stored and often trapped emotions,

202

trauma and wounds. We also tend to store a lot of negative or harmful beliefs which we are completely unconscious of. We may be holding on to things which do not belong to us, keeping us out of alignment and entwined in beliefs, realities, stories or "frequencies" which are harmful to self. Anything which brings us back into our body and thus back into our instinctual essence and "gut," therefore, can bring great inner balance and harmony. Due to the fact that emotions and higher realms and channels of thought and feeling, such as the intellect, our intuition and higher self holistically, are deeply connected to our lower self (gut/stomach/primal instincts); this naturally means balance is activated, and the body's self- healing mechanisms initiated!

To balance the Heart centre....

Daily affirmations, mantras, self- healing activities and exercises, any sort of therapy and spiritual healing are all effective for healing the heart centre. Meditation, learning a Healing Art, receiving energy healing (like reiki) and paying attention to your dreams are fine routes too. Dreams link to the subconscious mind and self, and this is where deep insight and healing light can be found. By listening to the key guidance and wisdom in dreams, we naturally begin a process of self-discovery and healing. Dreamworlds are just as important as waking life; we have both a moon and sun, after all. Darkness and lightness permeates all of life. The heart is the centre of consciousness. It links the lower self and higher self, thus acting as a bridge, of sorts, between lower consciousness and higher consciousness. Heaven and earth. The divine and primal, or animal. The heart is a central point and link to empathy, self-love, compassion, unconditional and universal love, and qualities such as tolerance, understanding, non-judgement and acceptance. We may sound like a broken record, but meditation truly is one of the most effective ways to heal yourself.

Receiving guidance and counselling can also assist you. One of the best ways to balance your Heart centre is to spend time in nature. Connecting to the elements creates powerful feelings of grounding and security and feeling at one with the world, and yourself. Elemental energies also assist in balancing your emotions, inner mental thought processes regardless of how chaotic they may be, feeling at ease and at peace with yourself, and increasing vitality. A lot of imaginative and artistic self-expression and ideas can arise from being in nature. Become an observer of your thoughts and emotions as they will fill you with the emptiness necessary for self-awareness and growth. Nature increases our flow of chi, the universal life force energy responsible for health, vitality and well-being- and our spiritual awareness. *Chi* is the force many ancient kung masters and martial artists work with to develop their internal strength, core being and inner spirit! You can cultivate empathy or seek to embody mindful empathic communication, which can be extremely catalytic to balancing your heart centre. Communication is the foundation of all relationships, soul ties and bonds. Without communication- either verbal or through our intentions and subtle impressions, we would not be who we are. Communication defines us; it is essentially us. With mindfulness and empathy combined any lingering issues in your emotions, interactions or intentions towards others can be healed and harmonized. You can further start to accept the parts of yourself you may have blocks or feelings of shame about.

To balance the Head centre...

Intellect, reason, rationality and logic can all be connected to and developed for balancing the Head centre, as these are the key qualities which lead to its balance. Intellect, planning, mental organization, problem-solving... any and all of these should be cultivated through mindful meditation. Mindful meditation is where you meditate with a specific focus and intention, for example if you choose to meditate on cultivating problem- solving skills you would set an intention and use a combination of breathing and visualization techniques. Meditation is simply contemplating and "going within" to increase self- awareness, and bring an expanded state of awareness and presence into daily life. You can engage in it to develop mindfulness, become the observer of your thought processes and emotions, and expand spiritual awareness. When used with visualization, you can further visualize the quality or skill you wish to embody and enhance and use natural laws like the Law of Attraction (LOA) to amplify your manifesting abilities. The LOA works on the principle of frequency and vibration, everything in this physical universe holds a specific pattern or encoding of information and through techniques like visualization and intention setting, you essentially utilize your thoughts and mental power to "project" an intended vision for future manifestation. This mental projection influences reality through the power of the subtle energy in place.

Your Head centre can also be balanced through connecting to your third eye and crown chakras and further integrating the qualities associated. Writing or journaling is a highly effective method to express your thoughts and expand your intellect, whilst simultaneously sparking your memories to help you in other areas. You may choose to educate yourself on the Enneagram, or at least your own Personality type, and write down all you can remember. Alternatively simply copying the wisdom and information contained can assist in activating your mental capabilities and taking you out of your body or feelings, and into your head. If you feel yourself to be too emotional or "watery," a particular emotional quality, then why not work to increase your inner fire or inner air? The air element is associated with communication, the mind and all sorts of mental abilities, including the ones expressed above. Air can be cultivated through spending time in nature, specifically in the fresh air, and watching birds or working with divination; the divinatory arts. It may sound a bit "woo" or "out-there," but have you tried trying to make a feather levitate through the power of your mind?! Regardless of whether you can actually do it or not, the sheer intent and mental power and capacity for belief alone will trigger your neurons in new and transformational ways...

Enneatype Compatibility

In this final section, we explore compatibility between the 9 enneatype personalities. This is just a general breakdown of what to expect. We may create another book on this topic for an in depth analysis later!

Type 1 and Type 1

This is a great match of two idealistic personalities coming together. There is star quality here- the capacity for soulmate and power couple potential! These two are defined by purpose, self-control and a strive towards perfection, always creating something inspiring and wonderful for others to benefit from. They're both conscientious and ethical, however need to watch out for criticising each other or projecting their own self-doubt and cynicism into their relationship. There's a tendency to nitpick and judge. Positively, 1 and 1 inspire one another to be the best people they can be, live with integrity, and go after their goals & dreams. On the whole this is an excellent pairing with true love potential.

Type 1 and Type 2

1 and 2 is a beautiful partnership full of inspiration, love and support. Type 1 deeply appreciates 2's wholly empathetic, sincere and loving nature. 2 pushes 1 to go after their visions and dreams, and is always there to empower them and give them the boost they need. Type 2 equally loves having someone to care for and nurture. On the whole, this is a positive relationship with many opportunities for love, kindness and affection. However, they need to be careful; 2 can become too possessive and people-pleasing, thus sacrificing their own needs over time. 1 may become impatient at this behavior while craving it simultaneously, thus leading to resentment. Honesty and open communication are needed for this to work.

Type 1 and Type 3

This pairing is full of vitality, passion and power... 1 is the idealistic visionary while 3 is the success-oriented achiever. This can be a match made in heaven, but it's not without its rocky patches and growth. Both 1 and 3 possess diplomacy and a strong sense of wrong and right; they both enjoy inspiring others too, so the limelight is a place they can both shine. There is real power couple potential here. Ambition, energy and charm define this relationship, so there's a lot of excitement and high-spirits which leads to much joy and positive connection. Negatively, the bond can become a bit too tense and unstable due to both enneatypes being high-strung, in different ways.

Type 1 and Type 4

This is a confusing pair that requires a lot of love and sensitivity to make work. They both share a love of the arts, creative expression, and striving for something greater than themselves. Type 1 draws their inspiration from their well-developed morals and desire to create change in the world; type 4 is similar but often goes into themselves, becoming the arty and distant type. Positively, 4 inspires type 1 through their advanced creative and artistic gifts. 1 equally provides 4 with the passion and respect they need to be their best. So, they support and empower one another. Yet, 4 is the most sensitive and withdrawn enneatype and this can frustrate type 1, especially when they're so critical anyway. Type 1 needs to develop extreme patience and sensitivity for this to work, and potentially accept 4 as their personal muse.

Type 1 and Type 5

There's a lot of conflict in this relationship and they always seem to be at odds with one another. Type 1 is an idealist with a direct approach, while 5 is very, very cerebral. Communication will be tricky and they will seldom understand each other, unfortunately. This is an excellent match in business and shared mission- creative and artistic projects thrive with this pairing! Just not so much in romance. They simply have different needs. As a 'Head' type, 5's require intellectual and mental connection and can often withdraw which conflicts with 1's need for perception . On the highest of levels, they both share visionary qualities, so this can connect them. Ultimately 5 is a bit too secretive and isolated for 1, and 1 is too partnership-oriented for 5's independent nature.

Type 1 and Type 6

This can be a great match, although it's not without its opportunities for growth. *Similarities*: they're both committed and responsible; they crave security and becoming exemplary human beings. Not so positive, 1 can be critical and impatient while 6 is prone to defensiveness and evasiveness. In saying this, due to being so perfectionist, purposeful and courageous, there is mutual respect and even adoration. Each admires the other's capacity to put the ego aside to be a champion for people in need, or the planet. Both are sincere in their motivations for a loving, peaceful and harmonious world, thus respect is gained. True balance will arise when they can accept their own and each other's follies.

Type 1 and Type 7

Type 1 will be the rock in this relationship. There are many strengths to a 1 and 7 pairing- they both have lots of energy and passion for starters. They also have an optimistic, high-spirited and responsive attitude. So, if their lifestyle keeps them on the go and active this can be a mutually benefitting and supportive bond. *However*, that is all it may be, a bond. Type 7 is the most impulsive and restless enneatype and 1 is the second most impulsive. There is not much staying-power here. If they can learn to be wholly honest and communicate their needs and feelings, there could be some potential. Type 1 would be the 1 pushing 7 to focus and apply themselves, make use of their talents, and be more mindful of their real-world commitments and responsibility, however. Positively there's a lot of joy and chemistry available.

Type 1 and Type 8

If anyone can tame an 8, it's 1! This is a rare pairing and one with immense power and potential. As the Reformer and Idealist, type 1 shows 8 the true meaning of being a conscious and inspiring visionary. They do so in a way that is both modest and graceful and self-authoritative and bold, and type 8 digs this. This could be an amazing match if they're both willing to learn from one another. They both have their flaws & follies, and this provides a mutual understanding too. 1's critical and impatient nature matches 8's domineering and confrontational one, in a way. The secret is they both crave love and harmony, therefore there is a mutual agenda for love and commitment. The key to success is to be aware of the other's demons and not feed them; show compassion and patience while they grow and learn together (and of course take on the world!).

Type 1 and Type 9

Type 9 is very agreeable and trusting. Type 1 is inspiring, courageous and charismatic *with* strong morals. They know right from wrong. This is a beautiful pairing with lots of wonderful moments of harmony, connection, and mutual respect. The Reformer and the Peacemaker even sound lovely together... They motivate each other to be the best versions of themselves; being the number of completion, 9 is all about self-mastery and unconditional love- type 1 cherishes this in a potential partner. This is an altruistic couple with a shared love of humanity, idealistic interests, and genuine intentions to make the world a better place. Both are capable of healthy levels of sacrifice to accomplish their missions, so they support and help one another. 1 further appreciates 9's nurturing, caring and gentle character, and the fact they don't demand change or perfection. This enables 1 to be themselves without being overly self-critical. Tips for success? Spend time alone to re-find yourself every once in a while.

Type 2 and Type 2

Type 2's together are magnetic and unconditionally loving. They ooze compassion, understanding and acceptance and are more than happy to please one another. There's a lot of love and support here. They're generous, sincere, warm-hearted and wonderful lovers! Yes, it can be clingy and possessive at times, they're both prone to codependency; but because they are so similar they reflect back their positive and negative qualities. Type 2 and 2 together act as a *mirror*. Essentially, this means they see themselves reflected back in each other's soul, and because there is only love, empathy and acceptance they can discover their "follies" and change. There's a lot of self-development available in this pairing.

Type 2 and Type 3

Type 2 and 3 can be a wonderful love match, there's a lot of joy, inspiration and laughter available. But, there are some fundamental differences they will need to find balance between to make this work. 2 is more sensitive and introverted- they display many qualities of the 'empath nature;' yet 3 is quite extroverted. They are the perfect example of "opposites attract" and there are many qualities they love and cherish in the other. 2 admries 3's pragmatic, self-assured and energetic approach to life, while 3 adores 2's caring, generous and flattering character. 2's will naturally want to give a lot of love and compliments to 3, and this is very welcome! The only thing they need to be careful of is falling into a narcissistic-empathic entanglement or karmic energy. If they can learn to balance the need to give (2) and receive (3) equally this can be a prosperous and long-term relationship.

Type 2 and Type 4

The main problem with this bond is that there is a strong chance 2 will slowly become 4's personal therapist or counsellor. Being so people-pleasing and giving means 2 will start to give too much of themselves, feeding off of type 4's need and desires for 'saving.' It can become a battle where they both fall into codependency and depression & melancholy- 4 more obvious and with 2 suffering in silence. This could work with complete self-awareness and honesty from both partners, however they would need to draw strong boundaries and commit to the light. If either one of these partners are of fire or air (astrology sun signs) there is a much better chance for success! Positively there is some power couple potential, as 2 is the Helper and healer and 4 is the Individualist and gifted and creative visionary. There is a deep connection through music, art and divine inspiration (creativity, self-expression, the soul).

Type 2 and Type 5

As an intense and cerebral type, 5 quite likes 2's sensitive and kind, giving and empathic nature. 2 equally finds 5's curious and bright mind and persona attractive, charming even. There much synergy and harmony in this relationship. 5 is capable of great vision and innovation while 2 is naturally steered towards artistic & imaginative outlets, being so sensitive and all… Things they need to work on: 2 will sacrifice themselves and their personal or emotional needs for 5's career. 5 will become secretive and isolated when they feel any sort of discord or disharmony. For it to work transparent and open communication is a *must*. In saying this, they will feel a psychological, emotional and even spiritual bond with each other that has the potential to lead to a lasting relationship. In business and friendship this is an excellent pairing.

Type 2 and Type 6

There is a strange type of synergy here that equates with unconditional love and universal compassion. They're both sensitive and feel supreme compassion and affection for one another. Type 6 is very loyal, reliable, responsible and trustworthy; being so sensitive, 2 is equally trusting and trustworthy simultaneously. Longevity can be established in a 2-6 pairing. When 6 becomes defensive, 2 knows how to respond to this type of trigger-trauma response with humility and patience. 6 admires this. 6's anxiety and rebellious tendency (acting out, etc.) is treated with care and compassion, a gentle type of understanding. This also pushes 2 to self-evolve and let go of their tendency to appease and please... Overall this is a warm and supportive match with opportunities for growth, mutual understanding, and self-development.

Type 2 and Type 7

Surprisingly, there is great soulmate potential here. You would think 7's impulsive and frivolous nature would result in a short-term fling, or 2's feelings being obliterated and destroyed- but this isn't necessarily the case. 2 and 7 appreciate each other's strengths, as they both have what the other lacks. Secretly, deep down, 7 craves companionship; they also crave compassion, someone to see their follies and inability to commit and love them through it anyway. *Love is a healer*. And no-one knows this better than type 2 (except for 9!). There's no chance of 2 falling into servitude or extreme sacrifice either because 7 doesn't need this. 7 is more than happy to show their feelings, independence and impulsive side. It's then up to 2 to decide whether this works for them or not.

Type 2 and Type 8

For this relationship to work, type 2 would have to be 8's silent and behind the scenes support system. There is a lot of admiration and respect available here. 8 is clearly the leader-they're dominant and success-oriented with a thriving career, most likely. 2 is a natural healer, helper and unconditional support system, so this could work *if* they're both happy to play their roles. Overall, 8 appreciates someone with sensitivity and emotional intelligence to come back home to, and 2 is more than happy to provide endless love and support. Because 8 will most likely be in an active career that takes up sufficient time, 2 is then given the space and time needed to enjoy their own talents, hobbies and passions. This is quite a harmonious and mutually insightful match surprisingly! *One major negative*: 2 needs to learn how to stand their ground and assert themself, but this can be learnt through their partner (8).

Type 2 and Type 9

When the Peacemaker and the Helper come together, this is a divine, blissful and harmonious union indeed! There is so much love, mutual support, understanding and sentimental emotional awareness of the other's needs, desires, strengths and follies-

and both have unwavering compassion and empathy for the other. Thus, this has 'holy union' potential; soulmate, true love, etc... Not so positive, codependency can be an issue. They tend to get lost in one another, both are sensitive with shadow traits including loss of self. The lucky thing about this is that in both of their desires to keep the peace and 'follow,' they accidentally form a unique type of synergy and subtle, loving, agreement. It's all about give and take, balance, and a continual recognition of what it takes to work.

Type 3 and Type 3

This is a very high-spirited love match which is also fabulous for friendship, business, and any type of platonic partnership. There is so much energy and drive that they could every well become a power couple. 3's "bounce " off each other and love the other's ambition, charisma and life force. They can inspire one another and keep each other on track, focused and committed to their dreams and aspirations. They need to be careful of superficiality and the jealousies and insecurities that naturally arise with such a high-spirited connection, however. It's easy to fall into competitiveness with either eachother or other men/women who they feel envious about. The connection can be quite intense! Lots of chemistry…

Type 3 and Type 4

This is another real 'yin and yang' or opposites attract relationship. 4 is more sensitive and reserved than 3, but they're both ruled by emotions, empathy and the inner worlds. They both prefer to feel out people, situations and their partner, and they both possess incredible levels of inspiration and creativity. So, on the whole this is a harmonious and positive love pairing. They do need to be mindful of their sensitivities, however; 4 can be vulnerable and resort to self-indulgence or melancholy while 3 is prone to bouts of self consciousness. In saying this, they enjoy each other's company and share many similar passions, interests and hobbies.

Type 3 and Type 5

This is a rather odd pairing yet one that can lead to a happy and long-term relationship. 3 is emotional and sensitive while 5 is cerebral and prefers mental connection. So, there are clear differences in the way they prefer to connect and communicate. Nethertheless, one is an Achiever whilst the other is

Investigator, so there's considerable potential for inspiration and helping the other succeed. 3 appreciates 5's ability to observe the world in an intelligent, subtly aware, and innovative way; 5 loves the fact that 3 is so driven and ambitious. There is a natural chemistry and sparkle between these two. To make it work they need to understand that they function on fundamental different frequencies, i.e. 3 is emotional while 5 is cerebral/mental.

Type 3 and Type 6

Another case of opposite characteristics and qualities can complement each other, 3 and 6 are generally considered compatible. Type 6 is extremely hard-working, responsible and trustworthy- they require security and commitment, and enjoy quality time with a lover and partner. 3 is driven, energetic and optimistic; they shine bright when they have something to focus on. Thus, they inspire one another and provide mutual support when needed. Issues may arise when either partner places their work above their relationship, but balance and compromise can overcome this pretty easily. The 6 shadow trait of resorting to rebellion and defiance teaches type 3 patience, empathy and poise which can help them achieve their goals. 3's tendency to become a workaholic can be eased through 6's modest and loyal nature, and of course sound advice!

Type 3 and Type 7

There could be some major issues in this relationship for a number of reasons. There is a lot of upbeat energy in this pairing, so tension and suppressed resentments could accidentally slip through. 7 is very impulsive and impatient while 3 is self-consciousness- this spells disaster! 7 doesn't give 3 the care and understanding they require, and 3 is too proud and self-focused to ask for it. Also, there are fundamental differences in motivations; 3 is concerned with helping others, such as achieving success or mastering a talent or skill to then shine for humanity's sake. Yet, 7 is more concerned with instant gratification and the thrills of the next best experience... Yes, there is possibility for inspiration, magic and sizzling attraction, but it's not without its shortcomings. If type 7 can learn to overcome their shadow traits this could be a deeply fun, joyous and vibrant relationship with lots of growth.

Type 3 and Type 8

There is a major clash here; both partners want to achieve success, yet they would rather give their all to their career and talents than to their relationship. Where's the compromise? Someone has to learn how to release control and make sufficient sacrifices for this to work. In saying this, there is a powerful magnetic attraction between 3 and 8. They both have a lot of love to give and can further appreciate the other's talents; respect and mutual understanding is certainly present. The key to success is to know right from the start that they are both equally ambitious & determined, and that neither one's personal aspirations or goals will ever be sacrificed. If they can find harmony and synergy this can be a very strong and inspiring couple. They may even join skills or forces to accomplish something amazing, something game-changing.

Type 3 and Type 9

This is a positive love match with many opportunities for personal development, growth and self-evolution. Each partner inspires the other and has something to learn through their mirror. 3 teaches 9 how to apply their talents and passions in a grounded and practical way; 9 shows 3 that they're on the right path by confirming their intentions for their desire for success and accomplishment. There is an underlying vibration or frequency of unconditional love, universal love, and a desire to transcend karma. Shadow work may come up- they will certainly find out new things about themselves! But, overall, there is no reason why this bond shouldn't work. Soulmate potential for sure.

Type 4 and Type 4

This is essentially the same as two water signs coming together, if you know anything about astrology… Senstiivty, empathy, moodiness, unconditional love and receptivity defines this relationship. 4's are romantic, self-expressive, slightly dramatic, and artistically and imaginatively gifted. They love to love and are more yin and fmeinine than most enneatypes. Commiting to self-growth is important for this to work. Being dedicated to their own healing path means they can reflect and mirror positive qualities, thus not giving into the shadow aspects of their personality. There's a chance to feed each other's light just as they may feed each other's darkness. Mindfulness, honesty and self-awareness are necessary.

Type 4 and Type 5

Despite being ruled by different primary forces, 4 and 5 are very similar. They share many characteristics and favorable qualities. 4's are self-aware, sensitive, honest and creative; 5's are imaginative, insightful and perceptive, and prone to introversion. Ultimately, they feel comfortable around each other and safe to be themselves. Because 5 often falls into melancholy and isolation, this actually inspires 4 to transcend their own self-pitying tendencies. They find inspiration in their lover's sadness and shadow. Simultaneously, 5 realizes through their partner that other people suffer from the same or similar problems they do- and that they don't need to be so closed off or isolated. There is a beautifully twisted type of poetry about this connection. Positively, they can heal each other and remind one another of the light, beauty and positivity all around them.

Type 4 and Type 6

When the Individualist and the Loyalist come together there is a unique type of chemistry and synergy. 4 helps 6 connect to their emotional and sensitive side, while 6 allows 4 to express themselves intellectually and psychologically. 6 is so hard-working and responsible that it pulls 4 out of their shell; they can overcome hypersensitivity and over-emotionalism by being more practical and self-aware through stepping into self-responsible. And, 4 opens a doorway to be honest and open their feelings- through type 4, 6 can learn that it's ok to feel intense and even tricky emotions, and instead of reacting from defensiveness or anxiety (and thus devolving into rebellious behavior and speech) to communicate as a mature adult. Overall, 4 provides 6 the emotional sensitivity and maturity they need to shine and thrive.

Type 4 and Type 7

This is one of the worst possible matches, in love and in business or vocation. 4 is very sensitive and reserved while 7 is extroverted and brash. 7 will literally walk all over 4, hurt their feelings, and make them feel like their sensitivities are a weakness, not a strength. All of 4's insecurities come to light with a 7, and because they are prone to melancholy and finding solace in the shadow realms, they almost get off on the suffering and pain. There's a sense of 'hopeless romantic' or 'vulnerable artist' with 4. This is worsened with the fact that these two enneatypes share artistic and creative passions, so it would initially appear like they're compatible. The only way this would work is if the 4 was very, very balanced and whole within, mature and older for example, and saw their partner as someone in need of imaginative inspiration.

Type 4 and Type 8

8 is instinctive and 4 is emotional… 4 relies on feelings while 8 draws their power and awareness through instinctive and emotional responses. So, there is some harmony here. There is a type of magnetic-electric pull between these two; personal attraction is heightened through shared creative and artistic talents. Passions and interests tend to be similar, although 8 will always be the dominant force and 4 the passive one. If 4 is happy to be a behind the scenes support system, including being a personal muse (of sorts) and inspiring their '8' partner, this could work! Both are capable of loyalty and long-lasting commitment therefore they are holistically compatible. 8 needs to be mindful of controlling or overpowering 4 and giving them the respect they deserve. Also, 8 can help 4 make sense of their talents and abilities and further step into new levels of self-leadership- they feed one another in different ways. Both partners appreciate this dynamic.

Type 4 and Type 9

This is a beautiful match and very compatible. It is an intense love pairing and full of romance, sizzling attraction, respect and admiration. They appreciate one another's outlook on life and enjoy the support and emotional connection that is given. 9'sare accepting, trusting, creative and optimistic while 4's are emotionally honest, creative, vulnerable and authentic. This is definitely a soulmate bond. The only thing they need to be careful of is falling into compliance. 9 wants to avoid conflict and keep the peace at all costs, yet 4 is naturally yin, receptive and passive. What does this mean? It means 9 may not always realize when it's up to them to take an assertive stance and steer the conversation or relationship. They both then unconsciously feed each other's insecurities and weakness at this stage. This can be overcome with awareness and a conscious effort to change.

Type 5 and Type 5

There is much inspiration and synergy in a 5-5 pairing. They're both very mental, aka cerebral, and they are both curious, independent, intelligent and perceptive. They observe the world with an open-mind and are flexible, in a sense. This means they're very open to discuss multiple viewpoints and listen to their partner's feelings. There's little chance of becoming dogmatic, tyrannical or argumentative in a destructive or separation causing way. They do need to work on their capacity for emotional bonding and also the tendency to want multiple partners. Commitment can be an issue, however they generally want the same things. Success is attained when they see each other as their best friend and mirror or reflection- their support system- instead of their enemy or rival.

Type 5 and Type 6

This is a very practical pairing with opportunities for commitment. 6 is loyal, responsible and practical and these qualities are appreciated by 5. 5 can be overly independent, they can be hard to pin down. Yet, secretly they do want a loving and supportive relationship. So, 6 provides 5 the staying-power and dependability they secretly crave. Because 5 is mental and cerebral they're also compatible- they're both ruled by the 'Head' (as opposed to the Heart or Gut). This relationship certainly isn't without it's difficulties, but it can stand the tests of time with open and honest communication and a dedication to stay faithful to one another. This is a great match for career or projects and paths built on an intellectual or academic foundation.

Type 5 and Type 7

5 and 7 are the most free-spirited and frivolous out of the bunch. This is a high energy, constantly moving and evolving, fun-loving and playful love bond. Both partners enjoy learning and absorbing new information, conversing about a range of topics, and expanding their mind and horizons. 5 is more curious, alert and inquisitive while 7 is spontaneous, playful and extroverted. Overall, it's a good match! The best word to describe this match is 'colorful.' Communication should remain open and transparent for success. 7 should also think twice before trying to outsmart, act superiorly, or lie and tell fibs to type 5; 5 will see right through it and be put off, because they are independent and pioneering above anything else. They have their own talents. Inspiration will be plenty in this pairing.

Type 5 and Type 8

Hmm… this can be tricky. 5 is insightful and inventive, curious and open-minded while 8 is very dominant and forceful. 8 has their own set of beliefs, opinions and skills which will conflict with 5's easy-going and open-minded nature. 8 will simply be a bit too dogmatic and self-righteous for 5. When 5 initiates a healthy and mindful debate, 8 resorts to confrontation and a different type of 'argument.' 8

can't understand how disagreement can be an opportunity to expand one's ideas and philosophies, or simply connect with another on an intellectual level. This makes 5 withdraw into isolation and solitude; at worst it makes 5 become nihilistic. 5 requires a deep intellectual and psychological bond which 8 unfortunately can't provide. And, 5 needs their mind stimulated and senses awakened through conversation, therefore it will seldom work.

Type 5 and Type 9

9 provides a tranquil and serene acceptance and peace to 5's life. 9 is comforting and non-combative- two qualities 5 loves. Simultaneously, 5 allows 9 to shine their strengths and best qualities without viewing them as weakness or follies. 9 is the Peacemaker, of course; accepting, agreeable and supportive- and type 5 enjoys the acceptance and non-judgement they receive. All 5 asks for is to be able to express and share their views and beliefs without criticism, to converse openly and authentically, regardless of whether everyone is incomplete agreement! 9 can provide this. Further, they're both creative with visionary qualities. *One area for improvement*: both can become isolated and eccentric, withdrawn or moody. They need to work on their communication skills and not worrying

about offending their partner, further combining it with developing thicker skin.

Type 6 and Type 6

6 and 6 are a match made in heaven. They're loyal, devoted, committed and security-seeking. They have the same values and love to work-hard to create a stable and supportive home environment. They're definitely soulmates with true love potential. This love match does need to be careful of defensiveness and reaction, however. Being so practical and hard-working means they tend to fall into negativity, anxiety and projection; they both let their frustrations out on their partner. It can become too practical, work or money focused, and grounded. I.e. emotional, spiritual and imaginative or creative connection may suffer. Working towards inner and outer harmony such as integrating other aspects of themselves will provide extra dimensions to the relationship, which naturally ease the stresses and constraints of being so dutiful and responsible.

Type 6 and Type 7

This is a bumpy match with moments of real closeness, bonding and harmony. Positively, they're both driven and open to a life of hard-work to reach success, prestige or accomplishments. This signifies a 6-7 relationship can last a long time, because they have other interests and passions outside of themselves. There would be a fine balance between their personal and professional lives, in this case. Not so positive, 6 is loyal and completely commitment-prone while 7 is free-spirited. There is a powerful discord and conflict of interests. 6 may occasionally have enough with 7's irresponsible and fun-loving, restless nature, and finally resort to rebellious and reactive behaviors (to try to make them see sense!). Yet, this doesn't work- it just pushes 7 to be even more of the things 6 doesn't like. So, ultimately 7 can't change or respond in the way they (6) would like them to. Effort and lots of patience is required to make this work.

Type 6 and Type 8

This is a very grounded and harmonious match. Both are practical, responsible, dependable and loyal; they both have a love of luxury, beauty, emotional connection and achievement, and they are clearly capable of working hard to create a stable and loving home and family life. This is a much better match than one might initially assume. 8 feels seen and supportive whilst not feeling overpowered or disrespected. 6 enjoys 8's confident, strong and assertive approach to life and their relationship. They both add something special to the bond. 6 is one of the few enneatypes who can show unconditional and unwavering loyalty to 8 through the challenges and hardships that arise. 6 is able to champion 8 and show courage and faith, and 8 digs this!

Type 6 and Type 9

Tranquil and down-to-earth, 6 and 9 are soulmates. This relationship is defined by a lot of love and deep respect, appreciation, and adoration. But it doesn't devolve into self-sacrifice or escapism, and this is because 6 is very practical and 'rooted.' The hard-working and responsible nature of 6 compliments 9's kind and compassionate, yet equally visionary and idealistic attributes. 9's shadow traits (follies) don't seem to affect 6,which allows 9 to shine and self-master themselves. This then inspires 6 to connect to their own inner visionary and inner spirit. All in all, they're compatible and help each other access their full potential. They also could very well step into a shared mission or service, skill or trade together with profound results.

Type 7 and Type 7

Excitement, passion, sexual vitality... spontaneity, fun, adventure... It's all fun, games and sizzling chemistry and sexual attraction. Does this bond have staying power? Who knows! But they don't really care either... 7 and 7 are partners in crime, two peas in a pod, and a bit scattered. They're a bit all over the place in all honesty, however there is a wonderful friendship and mutual attraction to be found all the same. 7's together are so extroverted and high-spirited that it can be difficult to talk about anything real at all, and this includes feelings, emotions and needs in intimacy. Wanderlust, a sense of 'living in the now' and open/free love defines this relationship, yet it seems to suit them quite well. The only issue arises when one of them decides to become grounded and responsible in their career or personal path, and the connection starts to interfere. Adult, mature and honest communication is called for then.

Type 7 and Type 8

Oh dear, talk about a toxic relationship! This is as toxic and karmic as a bond can get. The best analogy to use for this relationship is a toddler throwing mud or wet toys at their mum or dad while they try to work and submit a business presentation in time... the next morning. 7 is like a teenager in comparison to 8's maturity and success-oriented nature. 8 is simultaneously way too serious and decisive for type 7. The *only* ways this would work is if 8 took 7 on as their side project, seeing how far they could help 7 grow and step into self-responsibility and greatness. Or, if they were both after a solely sexual fling and affair... this could work. Lust and chemistry are about the only positives of this connection, and there's certainly more disconnection and discord than real and authentic harmony or synergy.

Type 7 and Type 9

Again, just like a 7 and 8 pairing this is not healthy. 7 will walk all over 9 and make them feel insignificant. 7 won't treat 9 with the respect and admiration that they deserve; they won't even see 9 as special, because there are fundamental differences in character. In 9's desires for peace, they will start to question themselves and fall into inertia and depression or despair. If these two really have their eyes set on each other, they will need to understand that 7 is extroverted and slightly selfish while 9 is balanced selfless. 9 has balanced their yin and yang yet 7 is predominantly yang. It could work if 7 sees 9 as their personal muse or an inspiring being to look up to, but 9 will equally have to accept that they will always be more evolved than their lover.

Type 8 and Type 8

This is a powerful, charismatic, mesmerizing and magnetic attraction and couple. An 8-8 bond is the definition of taking over the world and showing others what true love really is. 8's who choose to pour their love and passion into their partner naturally start to energize and increase their frequency, or overall vibration. This is because their partner's are mirrors of them, so reflecting positive qualities amplifies their inner light and 'sparkle.' Magnetic, multi-talented and affectionate, there are no heights two 8's can't reach when they join forces. This relationship is defined by charm, mutual understanding, support and loving attentiveness; they're loyal, devoted, faithful and protective with key skills in communication and problem-solving. Any negative attributes will be realized early on, as they both show each other what they don't want to embody (domineering, tyrannical, egocentric, etc.).

Type 8 and Type 9

Surprisingly, this sort of works! Because 9 is so accepting and all-embracing, 8 feels free to change without being judged. This is the key for 8, they have a real problem with vulnerability which prevents them from making sufficient changes in their life; they don't like to show 'weakness.' Yet, because 9 really doesn't judge and is the embodiment of compassion and generosity, 8 feels safe, comforted and protected around them. 8 can learn how to drop their guards while 9 vibes off of 8's assertiveness and strength. These two often flow effortlessly like yin and yang, or come to minor clashes but then grow and evolve together. Both partners are mature and emotionally intelligent, and any confrontation or intimidation 8 shows will instantly be watered down- deflected- with love and higher awareness. This is a soulmate bond.

Type 9 and Type 9

Finally, the Peacemaker and the Peacemaker... Like other same enneatype pairings, 9 and 9 are soulmates and compatible. The positive traits of being trusting, accepting, compassionate, supportive and inspiring are all mirrored back to each other. They are open to growth and personal development, and they both dislike conflict and unnecessary tension. They can experience long and happy, abundant and beautiful life together! The only thing they need to work on is assertiveness- speaking up and not becoming compliant, or complacent. Complacency (smugness, overly-proud) is birthed from insecurity and insecurity arises when they don't feel seen, heard, or understood. Thus, communication is the key to confusion. (This bond is also symbolic of a divine soul union partnership; two spiritually awakened beings working towards a common mission, or some humanitarian, selfless and charity goal.)

BONUS Chapter: A Powerful Meditation & Self- Healing Exercise

Now you are familiar with your Personality type, the subsequent Holy Idea, Virtue, Passion and Ego-Fixation, and how the Enneagram itself can be used to develop empathy, meditation and mindfulness; it is highly significant to *actively engage* in self-development in relation to the teachings and integrations of this unique system of self-discovery. Below is a simple yet powerful meditation and self-healing exercise, allowing you to connect to any of your positive and favorable personality aspects, and Holy Idea or Virtue simultaneously, to increase, enhance and embody each for intended effect. Knowledge is power, but the active application of the knowledge and wisdom contained in the Enneagram is what will really amplify and enable you to access its teachings.

Step 1: Creating A Sacred Space

The whole principle of the Enneagram is based on the concept of there being a divine and timeless reality. This can be confirmed through the frequent advocation of each of us being made of "Essence" and also having a soul; the soul is timeless and infinite and further transcends any perceived limitations of the physical realm and material reality we reside in. "Sacredness" is honoring and recognizing the sacred aspect of life, that there is a divine and spiritual reality awaiting us. But, this reality is not separate from us or something seldom reached, it is very close to us and easily accessible with the right willpower, openness of mind, heart and spirit, and willingness to surrender and let go; detaching from the physical body and opening our minds to worlds of limitless possibility.

A sacred space, therefore, is essential for a successful and profound meditation.

1. Start creating your sacred space by setting up a physically comforting and safe- feeling space. This may include cushions or soft pillows on the floor, and "clearing" your room or space before performing the meditation in it. Clearing is also known as energetic clearing, or energetic cleansing. It is about recognizing the subtle- spiritual

energy which flows through all living things, including our own bodies, and all physical environments. Your environment needs to be clean, pure and cleansed in order to experience this meditation exercise in its optimum. So clear and cleanse the room or physical environment, and *set some intentions* in the space, thus creating an element of *sacredness*.

2. Focusing on the elements, the elemental energy permeating around you is the next step. Earth, air, fire, water and ether- or spirit- construct physical reality as we define and perceive it. These elements flow through our own veins just as they flow through planet earth and the universe as a whole. Elemental energy is essentially in everything, from the fruits and soul-nourishing foods we eat, the water we drink and bathe in and the natural world we walk through. *Earth* can be connected to by having a crystal, special gemstone, shell or stone near you. *Air* can be present with a feather. *Fire* can be near you with a candle, and *water* can be attuned to with objects from the sea or a simple glass of water. For *spirit or ether*, any symbol which reminds you of the divine or any deity you pray to will suffice. Alternatively, you may have a picture of

some spiritual or healing symbolism, such as the 7 major chakras or some other ancient symbolism. Whatever helps you connect to the innermost core of yourself, to your essence; use.

3. Get comfortable and set some intentions. Intention setting is very important for this meditation to work, as through the power of intentions you project subtle energetic influences through your thoughts and essence. Intentions come from your truest self, your higher self and your heart and soul. When you set intentions from an aligned and sacred space you realize that life is a unified and interconnected experience, and that you can manifest things in harmony with your heart's desires when thinking, perceiving and acting from such a pure space. Our hearts give off powerful yet subtle vibrations, and the frequencies of our thoughts emanate these subtle vibrations. In short, we are powerful shapers and creators of our realities- both our inner worlds and outer external ones.

4. Next, make sure that the lighting in the room is such that it doesn't distract you. Too much or bright artificial lighting can be detrimental and interfere with your ability to connect to your intuitive, higher self-essence. Light

some candles, safely, or opt for a natural source of light such as a Himalayan Salt Rock lamp, or an eco-friendly LED Moon lamp. Alternatively, dim the lights or just have a small lamp nearby.

5. Finally, physically "cleanse your space." Organic and herbal incense, sage, frankincense resin oil, or an essential oil in an oil burner are all highly effective ways to cleanse your space. Sage, frankincense and a Peruvian wood called Palo Santo are particularly revered by many spiritual practitioners and frequent meditators.

Step 2: Define Your Intentions: What is the Purpose?

At this stage it is important to become aware of the purpose and what will actually be happening. This was briefly shared in the introduction, however, let's re-clarify and expand. This meditation allows you to connect to any of your positive and favorable personality aspects, and the Holy Idea or Virtue simultaneously. So, during the meditation there will be a technique of visualizing your intended quality or positive personality attribute and watching it grow or expand within you. The technique of visualization is very powerful, as on a subtle level intention, frequencies of thought and belief, and the essence and meaning you give something actually hold considerable power. There is a reason why the saying "dream something into being" has become so popular. It is because our minds are powerful tools and channels for manifestation.

Whatever you wish to amplify and integrate can be achieved through recognizing the influence and power of subtle energy and intentions. Your thoughts hold great impact and can be catalytic to your self-development and spiritual growth.

Step 3: Familiarize Yourself with Your Unique Holy Idea, Virtue, Passion and Ego- Fixation.

Before you officially sit down in your sacred space and get ready to go deep into meditation, it is very important to make sure you are completely comfortable and familiar with the essence of your Personality type. Read, study, learn and memorize. Why? Well, if you don't know what you are connecting to, or why, you won't be able to actually do it. Again, knowledge is power, and you need to make sure you are in the know. Know your strengths, weaknesses, gifts and talents, and shadow traits, for this is the only way you can use this exercise for healing, growth and personal transformation.

The Meditation

You may wish to record this on a mobile or recording device. Speak in a soft, compassionate and soothing voice, or just speak as if you are empathically giving yourself direction and guidance. This meditation can last from anywhere between 15 to 45 minutes, depending on how deep you wish to go and how long you feel comfortable being in such a transcendental space. Or you can just familiarize yourself with the meditation and engage in it without spoken guidance.

- Start by closing your eyes and going within. Calm your mind, still your senses, and feel safe, secure and protected in your body. You are protected and in tune with the world around and your inner being. There is only security, guidance and protection here, so begin to breathe and feel relaxed inside.

- Any tension or resistance that may appear is natural. The key to know with meditation is that a lot of past memories, pains, trauma and wounds can be (unconsciously) stored in our cells. This means that we begin meditation, if we are new to it, the process of conscious breathing itself and filling ourselves up with empty space can trigger natural tension. This is perfectly normal, so instead of resisting, panicking or feeling anxious or fearful, just focus on your breath and surrender. Any scary, negative or unwanted thoughts will flow through you just as your breath is flowing through you.

- Now you should feel more settled and content within, keep breathing consciously. With each inhale visualize a beautiful, gentle but warm and powerful golden light. This light is entering through your first center- your stomach region- and travelling up your spine, past and over your heart, and into your head. As it makes its way into your head, either in between your eyes above your brow or directly at the top of your head, picture this same golden gentle light making its way out of you. Exhale and see this healing light leave you. As it leaves, know that all tension, worries and concerns are leaving you- you are being cleansed with this golden light.

- Continue this process for 5-10 minutes, keeping your focus on your inhales with the light energy travelling up through you, from your gut, and spilling out into your head; to then be released through your exhale and along with it any tension and negative thoughts. At this stage, be mindful of your stomach, your gut and your center and its significance and symbolism. See this beautiful healing light filling you up inside, shining light and health on your Passion and Ego- Fixation, and any undesirable traits which may come with your Personality type. Like a DNA spiral, or a snake, visualize this same light with each breath making its way to the crown of your head, filling up the forefront of your conscious mind- your brow- and leaving you. Repeat this as many times as feels comfortable, and until you feel light and content within.

- Now you are going to *fill yourself up* with the quality you wish to expand and embody. This can also be called *energizing*- you are essentially energizing yourself with your positive and favored traits and characteristics. This element of the meditation can be done as many times as you want and feel comfortable doing, for example you may choose to start with your Holy Idea, then work your way onto your Virtue, and then finish with 2- 3 different personality strengths. For example, if you are Personality Type 9 you would visualize and project "love" (Holy Idea), "positive or empathic action" (Virtue), peace, harmony, empathy or compassionate and mindful communication (some of your qualities). *Empathy* can also be used for *all* 9

Enneatypes, and due to the purpose and intentions of this book, we will be sticking with empathy as a quality in the remaining guidance.

- Start by taking some deep breaths and reconnecting to your inner core once more. Set a brief yet strong intention of connecting to the quality or trait you wish to embody and amplify. See the word, connect to the essence of the quality, and mentally project a visual representation of it. Now, picture the word "empathy" (holistic example) in your mind's eye whilst breathing in from your gut. This time, visualize a beautiful green light growing and expanding from your first center- your gut- and travelling up your spine, through your heart and out into your Third Eye Chakra (energy center). As described earlier, this is the seat of your intuition, psychic or spiritual vision, and connection to the divine. It is in this energetic center where your consciousness can become activated in new and profound ways, and your beautiful qualities can be enhanced through visualization and mental imagery projection exercises. Continue to see this green light, linking to the heart and quality of empathy, energizing you from the inside. As you exhale, visualize the same green energy light leaving you and dispersing into the ether and spiritual realm around, with a subtle intention of releasing all that no longer serves you. You don't have to actively picture fears, worries or negative thoughts leaving you, instead just picture the healing green light whilst setting an intention for healing and release. This in itself will assist in removing any thought, feeling, emotion or belief not aligned with your highest self, whilst keeping the focus on the positive characteristic or personality trait you do want to energize.

- Once a steady flow has been created and you feel connected to the green light, begin to develop a deeper connection of the quality wishing to be increased and integrated. Start to envision scenes or scenarios in your mind's eye with the quality in focus. They don't have to be too complex, just make sure you connect to the feeling and essence of the visual representation. For example, for empathy you may picture yourself smiling with a warm glow around you whilst you offer loving and supportive words to a stranger. You may envision you actively engaged in a charitable or deeply helpful service or action, or you may see yourself walking through nature smiling at the birds, flowers and trees, in deep recognition of the conscious life force flowing through all living things. Any scene which resonates with your core and true self, attune to and align with.

- Stay in this energetic space connecting to the feeling for a few moments. Continue to breathe consciously, and with each inhale visualize this green, warming and comforting empathic light filling up the scene in your mind's eye.

- Now you are going to bring your hands up to your face, a few inches extending outwards, with your palms facing you. In many ancient and healing systems the palms are known as the palm chakras, and it is here where many healers and practitioners of healing energies channel energy and universal or divine power. Set a brief intention, and run your hands all the way down from your Third Eye/brow to your gut/stomach. The intention is to *cleanse* and *clear* yourself, bringing you back to point or ground zero. The purpose of this is due to the next stage in this self-healing meditation.

- Just like with "filling yourself up," this time you are going to *clear yourself* and heal your soul and psyche of your Passion and Ego-Fixation. Please note this is not about denying or repressing your Passion and Ego-Fixation, the intention is solely to transcend the limiting and self-destructive beliefs and energetic associations connected to it. For example, as a Personality Type 9 will be focusing on Slothfulness and Laziness, and how you wish to overcome these negative character traits. So, to begin, bring your left hand a few inches away over your gut. Hold it there gently and move it back and forward slightly, until you feel an energetic pull like a magnet. You should be able to feel this subtle magnetism quite powerfully at this stage in the meditation. Gently rest your hand, with your palm facing towards your stomach, a few inches away and bring your right hand up to your right shoulder. Keep your palm facing outwards and make sure the location of your hand is about shoulder's length, just above your heart. Take some deep breaths and start to feel a gentle force like a circuit between the palms of your two hands.

- Now, project and see your Passion shimmering from your gut and stomach, and slowly emanating out into your left hand's palm. Take some deep conscious breaths and with each inhale, visualize this Passion leaving your gut and spilling out into your

253

left palm, whilst keeping your mental focus on the intention of being free of it. As you continue to breathe in, see this unwanted Passion circling round all the way to your right hand and with each exhale leaving you. Watch this Passion flow through your right palm, spilling out into the ether where it will be healed, cleansed and released. Your Passion characteristic is being cleared and cleansed, leaving you with each breath. It is returning back to the divine where the divine's unconditional love and compassion is sending forgiveness, healing and acceptance.

- Continue to do this until you feel light, airy and with a content emptiness inside. You may be feeling an energy current or strong sensation now, or you may physically see swirls of light surrounding you or emanating from your stomach and hands. This is all completely normal, so just be still inside and know that you are safe, blessed and protected. In this energetic space all is well and you are loved, and cherished. Great and deep healing and transformation are occurring now.
- Repeat this with the Ego-Fixation and anything else in relation to your Personality type you wish to let go of.

- Finally, and to end this powerful exercise, become still inside once more, connect to your physical body, and bring your awareness to your physical surroundings. Keep your eyes closed still but be mindful of the sacred space you have previously set up and your physical environment. Become conscious of any physical sensations which may be arising, within or around you in your subtle body, and once again create some intentions. Thank the power of the Enneagram and the power of the universal energies which assisted you throughout, and finally bring your awareness to the sequence of visualizations and techniques throughout the meditation.

- When you are ready, open your eyes and know that you have just been blessed and filled with your Holy Idea, Virtue and beautiful Personality traits, and simultaneously cleansed and healed of your Shadow traits. All which no longer serves you are leaving you now and healing and transformation are still occurring on a deeper level.

Afterword

The Enneagram is a powerful system of healing and self-discovery. It compliments *Astrology* and *Numerology* beautifully, as we explore in the second and final book to this Enneagram series, although it is not as well-known as these other esoteric fields of self-study. The 9 Personality types can be used to explore deep into your core self, psyche and inner worlds, for deep insight and personal transformation.

In ***Practical Enneagram, Numerology & Astrology for Beginners*** we delve deeper into the world of the Enneagram.

Printed in the USA
CPSIA information can be obtained
at www.ICGtesting.com
LVHW022135290823
756688LV00005B/18